Real Life Financial Planning

with

Case Studies

An Easy-to-Understand System to Organize Your Financial Plan and Prioritize Financial Decisions

Todd D. Bramson, CFP®, ChFC, CLU

BOOK IDEA SUBMISSIONS

If you are a C-Level executive or senior lawyer interested in submitting a book idea or manuscript to the Aspatore editorial board, please email authors@aspatore.com. Aspatore is especially looking for highly specific book ideas that would have a direct financial impact on behalf of a reader. Completed books can range from 20 to 2,000 pages – the topic and "need to read" aspect of the material are most important, not the length. Include your book idea, biography, and any additional pertinent information.

ARTICLE SUBMISSIONS

If you are a C-Level executive or senior lawyer interested in submitting an article idea (or content from an article previously written but never formally published), please email authors@aspatore.com. Aspatore is especially looking for highly specific articles that would be a part of our Executive Reports series. Completed reports can range from 2 to 20 pages and are distributed as coil-bound reports to bookstores nationwide. Include your article idea, biography, and any additional information.

GIVE A VIDEO LEADERSHIP SEMINAR

If you are interested in giving a Video Leadership Seminar, please email the ReedLogic Speaker Board at speakers@reedlogic.com (a partner of Aspatore Books). If selected, ReedLogic would work with you to identify the topic and create interview questions. You would then have someone videotape you answering the questions. ReedLogic producers then cut the video and turn it into a segment that is like a seminar teaching the viewer on your area of expertise. The final product is burned onto DVD and distributed to bookstores nationwide.

Published by Aspatore Inc.

For corrections, company/title updates, comments, or any other inquiries, please e-mail store@aspatore.com.

First Printing, 2006
10 9 8 7 6 5 4 3 2 1

ISBN 1-59622-482-7
Library of Congress Control Number: 2006926904

Managing Editor, Laura Kearns, Proofread by Eddie Fournier

Material in this book is for educational purposes only. This book is sold with the understanding that neither any of the authors nor the publisher is engaged in rendering legal, accounting, investment, or any other professional service. Neither the publisher nor the authors assume any liability for any errors or omissions, or for how this book or its contents are used or interpreted, or for any consequences resulting directly or indirectly from the use of this book. For legal advice or any other, please consult your personal lawyer or the appropriate professional.

The views expressed by the individuals in this book (or the individuals on the cover) do not necessarily reflect the views shared by the companies they are employed by (or the companies mentioned in this book). The employment status and affiliations of authors with the companies referenced are subject to change.

Aspatore Books is the largest and most exclusive publisher of C-Level executives (CEO, CFO, CTO, CMO, Partner) from the world's most respected companies and law firms. Aspatore annually publishes a select group of C-Level executives from the Global 1,000, top 250 law firms (Partners and Chairs), and other leading companies of all sizes. C-Level Business Intelligence™, as conceptualized and developed by Aspatore Books, provides professionals of all levels with proven business intelligence from industry insiders—direct and unfiltered insight from those who know it best—as opposed to third-party accounts offered by unknown authors and analysts. Aspatore Books is committed to publishing an innovative line of business and legal books, those which lay forth principles and offer insights that when employed, can have a direct financial impact on the reader's business objectives, whatever they may be. In essence, Aspatore publishes critical tools—need-to-read as opposed to nice-to-read books—for all business professionals.

Dedications

This book is dedicated to our spouses, parents, children, siblings and many friends and relatives. Without the love, support, and guidance of all of these people, we wouldn't have learned the most important lesson of life..." When all is said and done, it is the quality and depth of relationships and experiences that are the essence of life...not the accumulation of material possessions."

Thank You

We extend a special thank you to...

...our clients who have trusted us with their financial decisions

...our support staff who help us to manage a complex business

...our business partners

Real Life Financial Planning
with Case Studies

Contents

Preface

I have gained wisdom, strength of character, integrity, empathy, and the value of giving by my parents' example. Unfortunately, my father passed away very suddenly at the age of 45, when I was just 16. It was three weeks from the day he discovered a few black and blue marks on his arms to the day he died of acute leukemia. In this short time, we never had a chance to talk about the future, although I feel his guidance through my conscience and in the wisdom of others, including my mother.

It is interesting how the experiences of childhood, both good and bad, mold the path we follow as adults. My dad did not have much life insurance, or any established relationships with trusted advisors. When he died, my mother was lost financially. She was given very poor financial advice and the small amount of life insurance she had was lost in an unsuitable and inappropriate investment. My family's misfortune defined my passion. It was through this unfortunate situation that I became empowered. My mission has remained intact for over 25 years as I decided this would never happen to my family or anyone who entrusted me with their important financial decisions.

Due to our significant financial crisis I became eligible for an Evans Scholarship. In the early 1930's, Chick Evans became a nationally ranked golfer and started a college scholarship program with his earnings instead of turning pro. This scholarship has now grown to the largest privately funded scholarship in the country. There are over 820 students currently benefiting from it as well as over 8,000 alumni. His vision and generosity has been an inspiration to me.

With that in mind, these books are my benevolence. I am now in the fortunate position of being able to give back. Some of the proceeds from this book will be given to charity, including the Evans Scholars Foundation, Breakfast Optimist Foundation, MDRT Foundation, Madison Community Foundation, St. James Lutheran Church, Leukemia Society, and many others. I am interested in "partnering" with other charities to help in their fund-raising efforts and I encourage you to contact me to discuss those possibilities.

I'd like to share a proverb containing some valuable wisdom and insight:

He (or She!) who knows, and knows he knows, is wise;
Follow him.
He who knows, but knows not that he knows, is asleep;
Awaken him.
He who knows not, and knows he does not know, is simple;
Teach him.
He who knows not, but does not know that he knows not, is dangerous;
Avoid him.

I believe it's our mission in life to listen to and learn from, or **follow** those who fall into the first category. But it is also our mission to take our unique gifts and make them available to those who are asleep or simple by **awakening** and **teaching** them. Also, time is too precious to spend with those who are dangerous. **Avoid** and minimize the amount of time you spend with people who fall into this category, and your enjoyment of life will multiply. We all have unique gifts and abilities and to the extent that our lives overlap and intertwine, we can all grow together carrying out our unique visions.

I am particularly grateful for the time, energy, and wisdom that all of the contributing authors have put into this book. This text is much more thorough and helpful with their input. The individual case studies in chapter ten provide an excellent summary and reference point for many situations. It is my hope that this book will educate, motivate, and help you to achieve all of your personal and financial goals.

Todd D. Bramson, President
Bramson & Associates, LLC
June, 2006

Tax Disclosure

1

The Basic Questions

Why the Title "Real Life Financial Planning with Case Studies?"

Collectively, we have spent almost fifty years working directly with individuals on their financial plans and financial planning questions. There is so much information to be found...but sometimes not much wisdom. Hopefully this book summarizes the wisdom we have learned and shared with our clients in individual meetings throughout the years. *Real Life Financial Planning with Case Studies* is simply a practical method of understanding, organizing and prioritizing financial decisions.

Most financial planning publications and financial plans themselves assume everyone lives a long, healthy life and saves a good portion of their income in quality investments that always do well. This book addresses all of the issues that happen in real life, and I hope you take the time to read this and work with a trained professional to develop a financial plan that meets *your* goals and objectives.

Why is there is an ever-increasing number of financial planning books on the market today?

Because there is an ever-increasing need to get educated.

- Few parents openly discuss financial matters with their children while they're growing up.
- Personal financial planning is rarely a subject taught in school.
- Many young people today begin their professional life already *in the red* when you consider the average college undergraduate student

finishes with over $20,000 in debt. (This does not even consider further graduate training!)

- We live high pressure, busy lifestyles that don't allow much free time to try and learn about all of the options that we have.

These unfortunate facts mean there are far too many people today who are ill-equipped to deal with the practical and fundamental necessities of planning for a secure and independent financial life.

Times have changed. Today, more than ever, your financial future needs you. Long gone are the days when you could rely on your company to pay back decades of loyal service with a comfortable pension plan. This is even more evident as we learn that some of America's largest companies report that their pension plans are under-funded. Many loyal lifelong employees are going to be surprised and even shocked when their financial security is in jeopardy. Even the government can't assure you of a reasonable retirement after a lifetime of social security contributions. Of course, social security was never designed to be the primary income for retirees. In addition, the financial products have become increasingly complex and we are continually inundated with confusing financial information.

These facts aren't meant to stress you out, but to wake you up to the financial reality of America today. It's not simply a matter of whether you will be able to retire rich, but whether you will simply be able to sustain your current lifestyle for the rest of your life.

Don't wait another day. This book is meant to give you an introduction into the often intimidating world of financial planning. You will learn of the varieties of investments and insurance options. You will begin to understand some terminology, and get advice on where to go to next, whether you intend to go the road alone or get some help along the way. Best of all, you will climb the pyramid of financial success.

Financial success isn't, as most people might suspect, the ability to make one or two decisions that turn a buck into a million. Rather, financial success is the result of many, many small but sound decisions that, when compounded, add up to substantial financial security.

You are in complete control. Or at least you should be. When it comes to spending and saving, investing and paying taxes, many may offer good advice, but you're the only one who can do anything about it. Maybe you're a chronic shopper. Maybe you're unsure of your investment options and how to prioritize them. Maybe you don't have a clue where your paycheck goes each month. In any case, if you're reading this book you already understand the importance of getting your future under control, and that's the crucial first step to financial freedom.

Who Needs a Financial Planner?

Financial independence and the accumulation of wealth are no accident. Granted it's not possible to plan for every single event in life, but even tragedy can feel more manageable when you are financially prepared for it. *If you're like many people, you probably spend more time planning for a vacation than for your entire financial future!* Whether it's preparing for the future, securing yourself and your family against tragedy or planning for the good times, your money deserves your undivided attention.

Car accidents, marriage, divorce, kids, corporate downsizing, death, retirement, for better or worse, are the realities of life. Planning for any circumstance, both happy and sad, may seem like a burden right now, but the right planning will rescue you when (not if!) unforeseen circumstances arise. Sometimes, solid planning can even turn otherwise bad fortune into good—maybe that downsizing could lead to a better job, or the divorce to a healthier situation, or the large credit card bill finally gives you the motivation to curb your spending and live on a budget.

The truth is, we all need to plan for our financial futures. So the question is not whether to plan, but how to go about making a plan, and whether we need a professional to help. The *information age* has complicated the field of financial planning. It is interesting to consider that twenty years ago financial news may have made top headlines two or three times throughout the year when the stock market would do particularly poorly or well, or if there was some other major economic news. Today, however, we have news programs dedicated to nothing else 24-7, and the number of financial headlines in the daily papers can be overwhelming. Still, there is a big difference between information and wisdom, and that's where the insight of a trusted professional can help.

Several situations which may call for a financial planner's expertise are:

- *You are a professional without much spare time.* If you're working for a large company, they may provide the groundwork for investing wisely for the long term. But even this process can't take into consideration the special circumstances of each individual or family. In this case a financial planner can save you a bit of your most precious commodity—time.

- *You are easily bored or overwhelmed by financial questions.* If, for example, preparing a budget is such a nuisance that you can't even imagine having to sort through anything more complex, like insurance options, trends in mutual funds or the stock market, then hiring a financial planner may be money well spent for greater peace of mind.

- *You are considering a complicated set of employee benefits in combination with personally owned insurance and investments.* You certainly don't want a new employer (or an existing employer who has changed their benefit structure) to conflict or overlap with your current investments. Such gaps or possible duplications should be examined thoroughly.

- *You are recently divorced or have lost a spouse who had previously been the one handling financial affairs for the household.* As if dealing with the trauma of divorce or death is not enough, being thrust into unknown financial waters without a trusted advisor can make you feel you're trying to stay afloat with bricks chained to your ankles.

- *You have recently graduated from high school, college, or grad school and are suddenly expected to become financially independent.* The saying "an ounce of prevention beats a pound of cure" is an important one in the world of financial planning. Seemingly insurmountable debt plagues the future of many young people. Learning to budget properly, to choose from insurance options, and to make wise investments are necessary life skills. Getting professional advice now beats paying for costly mistakes later.

- *You are self employed.* In this case, you most likely have to "wear many hats" as an entrepreneur. You are in manufacturing, sales, marketing, accounting, customer servicing, and probably don't have time to investigate or be aware of the many planning options available to you for you and your employees. A financial planner can help you sort through the many issues facing you.

As much as some of us would like to leave it all up to a professional, it's crucial that you understand the basics. A financial advisor is someone to educate and advise you and assist you in taking action to develop a plan, but ultimately the final decisions are yours. A good financial planner will educate you as to the options you face, acting as a teacher, so that you understand all of the relevant issues. A successful financial plan is an ongoing process that stays up to date with your situation.

There are many sides to most issues. The topic doesn't matter…whether it's religion, politics, stocks, insurance, sales loads, or how to finance your house…just to name a few. There are always many individual considerations, and the correct solution depends on a variety of factors. We are leery of advice that suggests you should "always" do this or "never" do that. We believe life is far more gray than it is black and white.

We are not the first to say this, and certainly won't be the last: "*It is crucial to trust your own judgment and instincts before taking action, no matter how good someone makes their argument.*" The best way to gain confidence in your own better judgment is to educate yourself on the topic at hand.

With that in mind, in this book, you'll find answers to the most important financial questions facing everyone:

- How much money should I have in emergency reserves?
- In which order should I go about paying off my debts?
- Which is the right kind of insurance for me & how much do I need?
- What are the most common financial mistakes people make?
- When should I maximize contributions to retirement plans?
- What is the best mortgage to take out?
- ....and many more!

If you don't know the answers yet, don't worry; just keep reading, because you're about to find out.

2

Where Do I Start?

Your Net Worth Statement

The starting point of any financial plan is to figure out your current net worth. This is a snapshot of what you are worth at an exact point in time. In order to determine your net worth you simply add up all of your assets and subtract all of your liabilities (debts). Sometimes, when you are just starting out, the net worth is actually a negative number because the liabilities exceed the assets.

In order to measure your financial progress it is important to know your net worth. Many people measure their financial progress by how much money they have in the bank. In reality, as the value of your assets go up, such as a house, business or investments, and as you pay debts down, your net worth may be increasing more dramatically than you think. The most important way to measure financial progress is to calculate your net worth regularly.

Don't panic! Here's where we have to get just a bit technical. Before you shake your head and think; *"Whoa, this looks way too involved for me,"* just try taking it one step at a time, following the chart and example below. After you learn how to do it once, it'll be just like riding a bike.

In simple terms, what would you be worth if you sold everything you owned and turned it into cash, then paid off all your debts? If this is the first time you're preparing a net worth statement, it's also a good idea to try and estimate what you think your net worth has been over the last few years. Hopefully you will be pleasantly surprised at the progress you've made.

Refer to the simple example of a net worth statement on page 21.

There are several categories within the net worth statement.

Fixed assets is the first category. Fixed assets are those assets that do not have a risk of a loss of principal. These would include the most conservative accounts that you can invest in. A few examples would be checking and savings accounts, money market funds, certificates of deposit, T-bills, EE savings bonds and whole life insurance cash values. These would be assets that you have access to in an emergency, they are available now and therefore are considered liquid.

Variable assets include most other financial assets. Examples include stocks, bonds, mutual funds, retirement plans, or any investment where the principal can fluctuate. Besides that, there is a potential for a higher overall rate of return on these assets, and are useful for the income and growth components of your longer term financial planning.

Your personal and other assets would include tangible assets such as your house, personal or business property, and vehicles. Other tangible assets such as a stereo, computer, camera, etc. would also be included here.

Don't get too bogged down trying to establish a value for every piece of personal property. You may already have that information available from your homeowner's or renter's insurance policies, but if not, a rough estimate will work just fine. The main reason for gathering this information is to have an estimate so that you can monitor trends. This way, when you are reviewing your net worth after some time, you will be able to track how this category has changed or to account for some of the money you spent.

Fixed Assets:

Savings Account:	$5,000
Checking Account:	$3,000
Certificate of Deposit:	$2,000
Total Fixed Assets:	**$10,000**

Variable Assets:

IRA:	$3,000
Mutual Funds:	$5,000
Individual Stocks:	$2,000
Variable Life Cash Value:	$4,000
401k balance:	$20,000
Total Variable Assets:	**$34,000**

Personal and Other Assets:

Home:	$200,000
Vehicle:	$20,000
Personal Property:	$20,000
Total Personal & Other:	**$240,000**

Total Assets: **$284,000**

Liabilities:

Mortgage:	$160,000
Home Equity Line of Credit:	$5,000
Vehicle Loan:	$10,000
Credit Cards:	$2,000
Total Liabilities:	**$177,000**

Net Worth: Assets minus Liabilities **$107,000**

Tip: Use a camera or better yet, a video camera to tape each room in your house, including closets and the garage. In the event of a loss, it will be much easier to remember for insurance company's reporting purposes.

For your liabilities, list the amount that you owe if you could pay off the amount today, not the total of the payments over time, which would include interest. Subtract your total liabilities from your assets to arrive at your net worth. If you're like many people, this can be a sobering experience. Don't forget to include all loans, like mortgages, auto loans, credit cards, student loans, personal debts, and consumer debt.

If you are young and/or just starting out in the work world, don't feel too upset if you learn your net worth is negative. For many people in the first stages of financial planning, it is the seemingly unmanageable debt that whips their spending habits into shape and pushes them to start planning for the future. It is also not unusual for recent graduates or those who have just finished some form of job training or other education to have a negative net worth because of high student loan debt. However, remember that education is not a needless expense and should be consider as an investment in your financial future. In fact, taking on debt to finance an education, a real estate purchase, or a business is an investment in your future, which should help you increase your net worth in the future. Consumer debt, when out of control, is what needs to be monitored and paid off immediately.

If you fit into the negative net worth category, your first financial goal is to get your new worth back to zero. For you, it is especially important to establish a financial plan and get control of your financial life as soon as possible. But, instead of dreading the process, have some fun with it. I suggest that clients throw themselves an *"I'm Worthless Party"* after they've worked hard to achieve their "$0" net worth. (Just don't put the party on a credit card that you can't pay off next month!)

Ignore the urge to put your head in the sand thinking you have no power over the situation. *You are not alone and there's no reason to be embarrassed.* To prove it you can take a look at our government. Their high federal deficit sets a dangerous precedent not only for our culture but also the world's economy. No matter how big your debt problem, it looks relatively small in this light!

Simply make up your mind now to reverse the situation and be proud that you're taking the right steps. The obvious way to improve your net worth is to decrease your spending and/or increase your income and savings. Begin by taking a serious look at your spending habits and make sure that you are doing everything you can to achieve, first a zero, and eventually a positive, net worth. Getting yourself back to financial stability may feel like a long and lonely road, but with the help of a financial planner you at least don't have to feel like you're going it alone. Or, why not "buddy up" like people do when they work out. Find a friend who is also motivated to get their financial act in order and educate yourselves and build your net worth together. After a while, being frugal, saving and investing, and getting on top of your finances becomes addicting.

The Millionaire Next Door by Thomas Stanley outlines some benchmark figures for what your net worth should be at any given time, age or stage in life. We'd encourage you to read that book for an in depth study of very successful people. Your net worth represents your financial security and ultimately, financial independence. So of course, the closer you are to retirement, the higher your net worth should be. A successful financial plan achieves one's maximum net worth, works under **all** circumstances, and maximizes the enjoyment of your wealth. It will also be important to insure yourself against unforeseen tragedies and to consider whether you want to leave an inheritance to your family or your favorite charity, creating a legacy that lives on forever.

In summary, the most critical starting point to a financial plan is evaluating your net worth. Then, on a periodic basis, you can compare the results in order to establish trends and measure improvement. A convenient time to do this is once a year when you're doing your taxes. This way all the paperwork is readily available and you're focused on your annual earnings and expenditures anyway. Keep all the financial records together from each year's tax forms and net worth calculations for easy reference.

Your Budget

After calculating your net worth, you'll want to look at your monthly budget and define exactly where your money is being spent. The categories of the monthly budget should also include any deductions from your paycheck like state and federal income taxes, Social Security, and employee benefits. Once you have your take home pay you should deduct all of the fixed expenses and the estimated variable expenses.

Are you unable to account for where a large portion of your money goes? This is the case for many people. To overcome it, try a few or all of the following tips.

- Carry a pocket calendar with you for three months and record every cent that you spend, no matter if it's for a candy bar or cup of coffee, or the mortgage and car payment. Then tally it up and categorize it at the end of each month. (Some software programs, like *Quicken*, make this very easy. Well…maybe not easy, but at least helpful. This process takes some time, but is well worth it if you are a spender.)

- Vow to go back to the days of *cash only* transactions. For everything other than your large monthly payments (and even those if you want to get really serious), stop using your debit and credit cards or writing checks for day-to-day expenditures like groceries, drugstore items, clothing, etc. It feels much different when you have to shell out $50 cash for a purchase than handing over a piece of plastic.

- Treat your savings account or investment amount as a bill that you pay out every month like any other. Experience has shown that if you don't get in the habit of saving money on a regular basis, either through a payroll deduction or an automatic withdrawal from you checking account, the money you intended to go toward savings or investments is mysteriously spent elsewhere.

How quickly you can move toward financial security depends on how motivated you are to saving money. It's not easy for Americans to live on less than their income considering our shopping and credit-loving culture. However, if you start early enough, saving 15 percent of your gross income will typically be enough to keep you safe from financial worries later on. If you are getting a later start, then you may need to be living on 75-80 percent of your income and saving 20-25 percent!

Keep in mind that saving or investing 15%, means you are able to live on 85 percent of your income. As elementary as this may sound, the significance is critical. In later years, this savings could accumulate to a substantial sum if invested properly. Also, it will teach you how to live below your means—a financial goal that seemingly every expert agrees upon, but few Americans live by.

3

The Pyramid

If you take a jigsaw puzzle and dumped all the pieces on a table, it is initially a daunting task to begin to put the puzzle together. Pick a puzzle piece out of the pile at random, and it is hard to know where that piece fits into the big picture. It is much easier to put the puzzle together when you have a picture of what the scene will look like once completed. So, you look at the picture on the box to give you a guide to what the puzzle looks like when completed. We designed the pyramid as a method of seeing how a properly designed financial plan looks when it is put together correctly. Once you understand that, specific decisions are easier because everything is in perspective.

The pyramid is a method of explaining the financial planning concept by categorizing your financial plan into stages. Of course, individual goals, habits, accomplishments, etc. are all unique, but most people share the same fundamental life stages. As a simple method of efficiently organizing your financial life, the pyramid represents the key to financial independence, and demonstrates the basic goal of increasing your assets and reducing your debt in order to have enough money invested to retire comfortably. Individuals may place more or less importance on one section of the pyramid than another, which is perfectly acceptable.

Without a doubt, organizing your finances in order to build a solid base is the first step. If you do this, you may be subjecting your financial situation to undue risk, which will cause problems later on. On the other hand, it's also important not to place too much emphasis on only one stage, neglecting the overall balance. This could be a sign of being overly conservative. As an example, not taking advantage of higher potential returns in equity (stock) investments may mean losing your purchasing power in the long run, because the dollars may be worth less due to the effects of taxes and inflation.

It is very important to try and accomplish a lifelong financial balance. You certainly don't want to get to the age of 65 with a huge amount of money saved up, only to be in poor health and not be able to enjoy it, especially if that means you scrimped and saved your whole life and worked so hard that you didn't enjoy yourself along the way. By the same token, you don't want to be nearing retirement and realize you haven't saved enough and now must take a substantial drop in your standard of living or go back to work to simply survive. The ideal situation would be to retire at the same or a greater standard of living than that you were accustomed to in your working years, but not feel at any time that you have greatly sacrificed.

As mentioned in chapter 2, a fundamental of short and long-term financial success is living on less that your income. If you can get used to living on 80-90 percent of your income, this allows you to commit 10-20 percent of your income to your net worth. Initially, this may mean aggressively paying of loans, but over time, the majority of this extra income should be saved. If you are living paycheck to paycheck, is there a way you can decrease your expenses, and/or increase your income so that you can start building some surplus funds into your monthly budget?

As you can see by the diagram, there are four main stages to the financial planning pyramid: *the Security and Confidence Stage, the Capital Accumulation Stage,* and *the Tax-Advantaged Stage and the Speculation Stage.*

PYRAMID OF FINANCIAL NEEDS

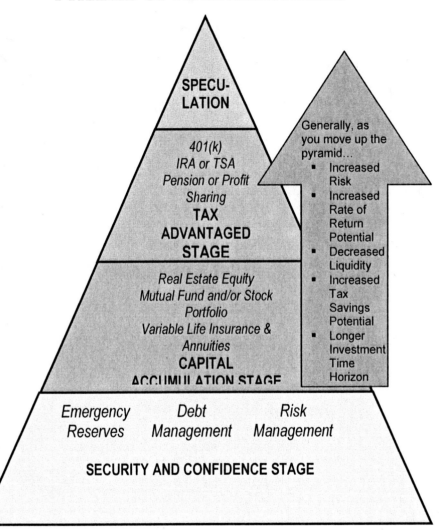

Generally, as you move up the pyramid...

- Increased Risk
- Increased Rate of Return Potential
- Decreased Liquidity
- Increased Tax Savings Potential
- Longer Investment Time Horizon

SPECU-LATION

401(k)
IRA or TSA
Pension or Profit
Sharing
TAX ADVANTAGED STAGE

Real Estate Equity
Mutual Fund and/or Stock
Portfolio
Variable Life Insurance &
Annuities
CAPITAL ACCUMULATION STAGE

Emergency Reserves   *Debt Management*   *Risk Management*

SECURITY AND CONFIDENCE STAGE

The ideal investment is completely liquid, has lots of tax advantages and a great rate of return and low risk. If you find an advisor or salesman claiming to have such an investment, you would be wise to walk…no, run away. This ideal investment does not exist.

Let's use an analogy of spinning plates. If you have ever been to a circus or seen a juggler (the Peking acrobats), you may have seen a performer attempt to spin many plates on top of long sticks…all at the same time. The objective is to take limited energy, and allocate it in such a manner as to keep all the plates spinning. It doesn't do any good to devote a lot of time to one spinning plate while the others are slowing down, wobbling, and falling down. The goal is to keep all the plates spinning!

Your financial plan is on somewhat the same level, with each financial decision representing a different plate. First of all, you need to find out which plates you want to start spinning and then direct your dollars to keep them going. You could have several debt reduction plates, some risk management (insurance) plates, retirement and/or college education plates, and so on. Each individual situation is going to be different. Again, there are limited resources that need to be allocated in such a way as to accomplish all of your goals. This is where the advice of a professional and experienced financial advisor can be very valuable. You can call us financial jugglers.

The key financial variables in the pyramid are risk, liquidity, rate of return and tax advantages. The money in your emergency reserves and at the *Security and Confidence Stage* should be very liquid or accessible. Generally, as you move to higher stages in the pyramid, the less liquid your funds become.

Risk and rate of return tend to go hand in hand. The higher the amount of risk you take, the higher the rate of return should be…given time. In the pyramid, typically lower risk and lower rates of return should be at the base of your planning with risk and rate of return increasing as you move up the pyramid. Historically, stock market and investing returns become more predictable the longer the time frame that is considered. Keep it mind, however, that past performance is not indicative of future results. (Compliance departments like that statement!)

From a tax standpoint, there are typically not too many tax advantages at the lower level. If you have money in a savings account, that money is generating ordinary income on which you are paying tax, so there are no tax advantages there. On the other hand, when you put money into a qualified retirement plan, the contribution is on a before tax basis, delaying and deferring the tax to a later date. Under most circumstances, however, you cannot touch the money in your qualified plan until age 59½ without paying a 10 percent early withdrawal penalty, plus the income taxes due on that amount. The rule of thumb on tax savings is similar to risk and rate of return. As you move up the pyramid, you'll have greater tax advantages on your investments.

A Discussion of Risk

There is no such thing as a risk-free investment, even a savings account is not risk free. Let me explain. Risk is commonly discussed in terms of loss of principal. This is market risk. Most recently, during the recent bear market of 2000-2001 (a period of downturn in the stock market), many investors lost some of the value of their investment if they owned stocks and/or stock mutual funds. There are other forms of risk besides market risk.

Purchasing Power Risk: Another term for this is inflation. If the cost for products and services rises faster than the interest rate being credited on your savings and checking accounts, then you are exposed to purchasing power risk. While you don't lose any principal, you are still losing ground relative to inflation. This is a particular problem currently for retirees who have traditionally held CDs (bank certificates of deposit) and lived off the interest each year.

Interest Rate Risk: Bonds and Fixed Income securities are subject to this risk. Your principal value can decline if interest rates climb quickly. The severity of the loss is often magnified by the duration and/or maturity of the bonds and the credit quality as well as how quickly interest rates rise. At this time, when interest rates are near forty-year lows, many people who own fixed income securities are unknowingly subjecting their investments to interest rate risk.

Business Risk: This is the risk of losing money due to circumstances out of your control. A business could go bankrupt, and your investment becomes worthless.

Liquidity Risk: This is the risk associated with being invested in real estate, limited partnerships, businesses and other investments where there is sometimes no immediate market for your value. This is problematic if you have a need for cash and you cannot sell or liquidate your shares. You would invest in something like this only if you had sufficient assets available besides this investment.

Regulatory Risk: Investors run the risk that government policy decisions or influences of society as a whole could endanger an investment's value. Environmental and tax legislation can have a dramatic impact on certain investment values, up or down. It is important to note this risk when investing.

Currency Risk: An investment in international securities can be affected by foreign exchange rate changes, political and economic instability, as well as differences in accounting standards.

Diversity Risk: This will be discussed at length later in the book, but allow me to overstate the obvious…DIVERSIFY!

In summary, a properly structured financial plan will balance all of these variables so that you are diversified by asset class, risk levels, tax treatment, and time horizon.

4

The Security and Confidence Stage

This stage is divided into three main sections with an emphasis on building up emergency reserves, making sure your debt is under control and taking care of risk management (insurance) needs. Each of these factors is equally important. Most people agree on the need to have money accessible for emergencies, to pay their debts, especially on high interest credit cards, and to be adequately insured. The trick to the individual financial plan is to figure out the appropriate balance and emphasis.

1. Emergency Reserves:

The one constant in life is that there will always be surprises. The purpose of an emergency reserve fund is just what it sounds like—money that is very accessible when you really need it. In fact, Will Rogers once said, "I'm not so much concerned about the rate of return on my money, just the return of it!" The main characteristic of an investment in this category would be the money that is liquid, yet safely invested so the principal remains intact. The most common mistake people make here is not having adequate reserves or taking undue risk with these funds. This money needs to remain liquid in case of unexpected expenses, like the car expenses, home repairs, job loss, or medical emergencies, etc. For most people, the benefit of having an adequate emergency reserve is access to funds when needed. When you are financially prepared for any surprises, they become less stressful and are therefore easier to deal with emotionally. Furthermore, when there is a source of funds for these types of emergencies you do not have to rely on credit cards, or personal unsecured high interest loans.

As a general rule of thumb, your emergency reserve account should be able to cover at least three months of bills. So, if your monthly expenses are averaging $3,000, then your emergency reserve fund should be $9,000. Of course, this is a rough guide and you may want to consider having a higher emergency reserve if you anticipate a big purchase, such as a car or home. Ideally, you do not want to deplete your emergency reserve completely in order to purchase such items.

It may also be important to consider an *emotional rule of thumb*—at what point would a drop in your emergency reserves make you feel nervous? Or, said another way, what is the minimum level of cash that you want to have? This amount differs for everyone and should take into consideration the stability of your job, your equity in a home, how large and/or liquid your other investments are, and any large bills or purchases you may be planning. If a large purchase or unexpected expenses do drain your reserves, then the emphasis of your financial plan should be to replenish those funds as a higher priority than your other investments.

The typical investments that can be used to hold your emergency reserves would include bank investments, money market funds, and/or insurance cash values. The common theme among these investments is their liquidity and the safety of the principal. If you use a bank for your emergency reserves, typically these funds are in savings accounts and interest-bearing checking accounts, as well as money market funds.

For safety of principal and liquidity, savings accounts are the most common option, but not necessarily the best. Such accounts are insured so there is no market risk, but lots of purchasing power risk. But, this also means there is typically a lower yield than other investments.

Another option is a CD (certificate of deposit), with a relatively short maturity. The disadvantage to a CD is that the money is tied up for the length of the guarantee period and removing the funds sooner will result in a penalty. To avoid this problem, it can make sense to stagger your CD maturities so that you always have some that come due every six months or so. Therefore, you can access it if you need to or reinvest if you don't.

A money market mutual fund is often the best choice as an emergency reserve possibility. Many people incorrectly associate the term mutual fund with high risk. However, a mutual fund only has as much risk as the underlying investments it owns. A money market mutual fund pools investors' dollars in the typical mutual fund style, and purchases jumbo CDs through banks, Treasury securities (T bills), as well as commercial paper. Most money market funds have check writing privileges, which allow you to write checks against your account, subject to minimums of usually $250 or $500. The rate of return earned on these funds will fluctuate based on the short-term money market, but is typically competitive with the interest rate at the time.

Investments in a money market fund are neither insured nor guaranteed by the FDIC, or any government agency. Although the fund seeks to preserve the value of your investment at $1.00 per share, it is possible to lose money by investing in the fund.

Life insurance cash values on permanent policies (i.e. whole life, adjustable life, universal life) can also be important sources of emergency reserve funds. These funds are typically earning a competitive fixed rate of return and they are accessible. It is usually possible to take out a loan or borrow against your cash value, using it as collateral; or sometimes you can take an outright withdrawal of this money. Remember, though, that any loans or withdrawals taken will reduce both your policy cash value and death benefit.

A home equity line of credit is another option. If you have equity in your house, and if interest rates are low and these loans are tax deductible, this option should not be discounted. In fact, in periods of time when there is a low interest rate environment, maintaining an open line of credit against your house equity can be a viable form of emergency reserve cash. It could also be used to pay down a high interest credit card or for a major purchase, like a car. The drawback is that it needs to be paid off when you sell your house, which of course would result in less money at closing. If your house would decline in value, creating less equity, you may have to pay off the home equity line and/or face a higher interest rate on the loan. While interest rates are higher than a few years ago, this may still be an option worth considering, especially if you can use the money to pay off higher-interest consumer debt.

2.   Debt Management

If you are in the fortunate situation of having no debts, congratulations! If you come from the school of thought that you don't ever want to owe anything to anybody, debt management is not an issue. However, in today's society this ideology is very uncommon and many people could use some strategies on effectively managing their debt.

Financially, it would make sense to rank all of your debts from highest to lowest interest, paying attention to the after-tax cost of borrowing. Since consumer debt is not tax deductible, those rates are taken at face value. However, a mortgage or home equity loan is deductible, so the real rate of return is the after-tax cost.

To give another general rule of thumb, credit cards and consumer debt would be the first to pay off, if they have the highest interest rates. Then you would want to work away at the furniture loan, the used car loan, the new car loan, student loans, (unless you have consolidated them in the last few years and the interest rate is five percent or less) and finally, the home mortgage. Nowadays there are many credit cards that offer very low interest rates on balance transfers, which can be a temporary solution. But beware that the rate after the introductory period is not actually higher than your current card.

It is also important to look at debt management from a cash flow standpoint as well as an emotional standpoint. With this in mind, it can make sense to pay off a lower interest loan if it will improve your cash flow dramatically, or if emotionally it is important for you to get it paid off for some other reason. Many people find a sense of satisfaction in paying debts off completely. Once one debt is paid off, take the extra cash and immediately begin paying off another loan more aggressively, so that cash does not get absorbed into the budget.

Check your credit report. It's a good idea to review your credit report every year. The financial information included in this report will have a bearing on whether you can obtain a loan, auto, or home insurance, rent an apartment, or even apply for a job. In addition, your credit score will determine the interest rate that you would be charged for your loans. Contact the credit bureaus and correct any errors you find. We would suggest starting at www.annualcreditreport.com.

3. Risk Management

Protecting yourself against unforeseen catastrophic losses is the third critical area of the base of the pyramid and the Security and Confidence Stage. In fact, think of this as a three-legged stool. Kick one leg out and the stool will not stand. The financial pyramid is just like that.

Important insurance coverage can include health and major medical, auto, life, disability, long-term care and homeowners or renters. In many cases, life and/or disability insurance are overlooked. However, these can be very important depending on your personal situation.

The reason for placing risk management at this point is obvious. You need to protect yourself from losses that would create such a hole that you may otherwise never dig yourself out. Then, once you are on your way to financial independence, insurance plays an equally important role in protecting your assets.

While you don't want to have any gaps in your insurance protection, you certainly don't want to overlap or duplicate coverage. The ideal financial plan will have you paying reasonable premium levels while providing maximum protection. Remember, the major role of insurance is to protect against catastrophic losses. A common mistake is trying to insure too many contingencies or not using deductibles to your advantage.

You will want to ask yourself a couple of questions before purchasing insurance:

- *Is the premium for this coverage going to dramatically affect my lifestyle?*
- *If I do not buy this coverage and suffer the losses that would have been covered, would I be in grave financial trouble?*

If the answer to the first question is *no* and to the second *yes,* then the insurance in question is right for you. If not, reconsider the structure and price of the insurance. Consult an experienced financial professional to help you determine the appropriate levels of coverage and how to structure your insurance within the context of a comprehensive financial plan.

When it comes to life insurance it is easy to become confused. Some complicated terminology like *term life, whole life, universal life, variable whole life,* etc. may put you off, but by understanding just a few terms and some of the benefits and disadvantages, you will be much more prepared to evaluate the coverage that is best for you. If structured correctly, life insurance can be one of the most versatile and powerful financial tools available.

- *Term life:* While the premiums are low for the young, the price increases dramatically as you get older. Although young couples with children may find term life insurance to be the only affordable option, it is important to remember that this option brings *no investment benefits.* To optimize value on the policy a *guaranteed renewal clause* allows for renewal to the policy without a medical re-qualification. Another value-adding option is a clause, which allows a conversion from a renewable term policy to a permanent policy without proof of insurability.

- *Whole life:* The most appealing feature of whole life insurance is its unchanging premium and guaranteed long-term coverage. Also, it builds up a tax-deferred "cash value." The cash value is what the insurer will return on cancellation of the policy. But, whole life costs more than term life initially. Some critics believe whole life's cash value grows too slowly and as an investment option the buyer is better off buying term insurance and investing the difference in the stock market. The policies' rates of returns today are much more competitive than in the past, and this can be a very viable policy for a portion of your financial plan.

- *Adjustable/universal life:* The main feature of this policy is the flexibility in initial design and the ability to change as your needs change. If money gets tight, with this type of policy it's possible to lower the annual premium. You can also increase or decrease the death benefit as your needs change. Typically, increases in death benefit require additional proof of insurability.

- *Variable Life.* The cash values are invested into investment sub-accounts with your choice of the allocation to stocks, bonds, and/or money markets. The policy's cash value and death benefit can increase if the investments do well. But, the opposite could also occur. Look ahead to the next chapter for a more advanced discussion of this type of policy.

Disability insurance is one of the most important and overlooked types of insurance coverage. The odds of a long-term disability (lasting 90 days or longer) are six to seven times greater than a death during working years. While many employers provide group disability insurance, the benefits are generally 60 percent of one's income and taxable. The net effect is that only 40-45 percent of your income is protected.

As retirement starts to get closer, and you are starting to plan for that, consider a long term care insurance policy. In some cases, we'll suggest that a person replaces their private long term disability coverage and use the premiums that are freed up to purchase long term care. The motivation is control (over the budgeting of this expense…and the delivery of health care in the event that you need this coverage) and protection of your wealth. We could devote an entire book to this topic alone. If you are in your late forties through your mid sixties, please make it a priority to visit with your financial advisor about this important coverage.

Remember, you get what you pay for. Searching the internet for the cheapest insurance policy often results in coverage that will not protect you and your family adequately. A competent insurance agent or financial planner can provide a valuable service and should be used. They can be the best resource in helping you to select adequate coverage at appropriate prices and at claim time they can help you decipher the paperwork. Choosing someone you trust, especially someone who comes recommended from a reliable source, will prove invaluable. Also, there may be some other aspects of your overall financial plan, which if reworked, can help you to maximize your insurance protection, while building wealth for the future using better strategies than you were aware of.

As your assets grow, it is wise to expand your umbrella liability insurance coverage. The limits built into most homeowners and auto policies are minimal. This coverage actually protects your assets in the event you or a family member cause harm due to your negligence. In addition, be sure to ask your agent for excess umbrella liability coverage for uninsured/underinsured motorists. This coverage protects you and your family for negligent acts caused by others.

In many cases, insurance is thought of as a "necessary evil." You have to have it but it only benefits you if you have a claim. We look at the insurance coverage we own as a valuable part of an overall comprehensive financial plan. The peace of mind we have by knowing our families and our property are covered is worth a lot. In addition, we can be more aggressive with our other savings and investments, because we know that our risk management needs are taken care of.

Looking back to the Middle Ages, we get a glimpse of the importance of insurance. People of wealth built fabulous castles and filled them with treasures. They always devoted significant resources to protecting those assets in the form of an army, a moat, etc. In a sense, that was an early form of an insurance policy. So, as you continue to build your net worth, you should review and update your insurance to be sure you are maximizing your coverage and protecting you and your family and your wealth.

5

The Capital Accumulation Stage

This stage represents a large amount of assets that you will build up over your lifetime. The assets that tend to comprise this stage are quite varied. Some of the investments include individual stocks and bonds, mutual funds, variable life insurance cash values, and equity in real estate or in a business. Aside from the equity that you build into your retirement plan, the majority of your financial independence will come from these investments. While these assets can also serve as emergency reserves, the investment horizon is usually five years or longer.

Keep in mind that all investments have risk. However, there are varying degrees and types of risk. The risk most often associated with an investment involves a fluctuating principal or a sudden depreciation in the stock market, as in October 1987, or the bear market of 2000-2002. A corporate bond or government security holds the risk of loss of principal due to an increase in interest rates. Even a safe investment in a money market fund has purchasing power risk, because after taxes and inflation are figured in, your dollars could be worth less than when you originally invested. A summary of the types of risk is found towards the end of Chapter Three.

Saving money is one of the most important criteria in assuring financial success. Get in the habit now of saving between 10-20 percent of your gross income. (10% if you are starting when you are in your mid 20's and 20% if you are over age 40) By living below your total income, even to this small degree, not only will your money be worth more in the long run by wisely investing it, you will also cultivate a responsible attitude toward your money. Keeping up with the Jones has become a national epidemic. But the real truth is the millionaires next door don't concern themselves with flaunting their wealth, which explains why they are wealthy. Some of the financial ideas and products that belong in the capital accumulation stage are discussed here.

Variable life policies are becoming increasingly popular. Because of their unique investment opportunities, their tax deferral potential and their excellent rates of return potential, this new type of insurance policy should be examined by anyone who is investing money at the *Capital Accumulation Stage*. Such policies allow an individual to purchase a single financial instrument providing for both life insurance and long-term accumulation goals. They often serve as a form of "forced investment" for those who find it difficult to put funds aside on a regular basis, but who routinely pay their bills. Obviously, your level of insurance needs and wants has a large bearing on how the policy is structured and it's important to carefully structure loans and withdrawals to avoid negative income tax results.

For many Americans, one of the most substantial forms of saving is simply making a monthly payment on your home. Generally speaking, real estate has long been a favorite investment tool for its tax benefits and as a buffer against inflation. Although there can be significant investment benefits in the long term, buying real estate is not without its risks. Deflation may decrease property values or suspected long-term growth in a given area may not occur. Changes in tax law may reduce or eliminate anticipated tax benefits. Also, real estate is not liquid, so the necessity of a quick sale may require a substantial reduction in price.

The term "stock" or "share" both refer to a partial ownership interest in a corporation, or equity. As a stockholder you'll be able to vote for the company's Board of Directors, and receive information on the firm's activities and business results. You may share in "dividends" or current profits.

Investors typically buy and hold stock for its long-term growth potential. Stocks with a history of regular dividends are often held for both income and growth. As the long-term growth of a company cannot be predicted, the short-term market value of the company's stock will fluctuate up and down. If your financial need or your fear causes you to sell when the market is "down" (also called a "bear market"), a capital loss can result. If the market is "up" (also called a "bull market"), the investor can realize a capital gain when selling.

While stocks represent ownership in a business, bonds are debt issued by institutions such as the federal government, corporations, and state and local governments. At the bonds' "maturity," the principal amount will be returned. In the meantime, bond holders receive interest. When first issued, a bond will have a specified interest rate, or "yield." If a bond is traded on a public exchange, the market price will fluctuate, generally with changes in interest rates.

Using a mutual fund is an excellent way to lower your risk, because you are diversifying through a number of stocks. A properly designed mutual fund portfolio is generally the most appropriate method of accumulating wealth at this point in the financial pyramid. Some funds have high "market risk," meaning they can fluctuate quite dramatically. Past experience shows that funds that have the most risk have upside and downside potential that needs to be carefully considered. Funds with low market risk often have "inflation risk." These funds usually produce lower returns which may not keep up with inflation.

If your investment horizon is relatively short (up to five years), then a more conservatively balanced fund, equity income fund, or even a medium-term corporate bond or government securities fund, will likely be the most appropriate. When your investment horizon is longer, growth-oriented stock funds are generally going to be the best choice. Again, each circumstance is different and the advice of a competent professional will be valuable. Most firms have a short investment attitude questionnaire which you can answer to help you determine the appropriate asset allocation strategy that meets your needs.

Diversify! Diversify! Diversify! Nothing else will be as crucial to your portfolio as diversifying and having a long-term vision. It's important to diversity not only by asset class but also by tax treatment and time horizon. We all know the proverb "Don't put all your eggs in one basket." Well, take it to the extreme—don't put all the baskets on the same truck and don't drive all the trucks down the same road! It's not necessary to look too far back to recall the faddish investing in technology and start-up companies of the late 1990s. Too many investors lost too much when the overvalued stocks plunged and those eager investors expecting big returns were left with substantial losses.

Sometimes misunderstood, the main goal of diversification is not to maximize your return, but to minimize your risk and lower your volatility. The basic premise is that there is as much risk in being out of the market when it goes up as being in the market when it goes down, especially for your long-term money. As an example, take the period between 1926 and 1995, a period of 840 months; if you were out of the market during the 30 top performing months—about 3.6 percent of the time—you would have ended up with a return similar to Treasury Bills! While diversification does not guarantee against loss, it is a method used to manage risk.

Some additional strategies to employ when investing include dollar cost averaging and portfolio rebalancing. Dollar cost averaging is the process of investing a fixed amount of money each month (or quarter, or year) without worrying about whether the market is up or down. When it is down, you will buy more shares, bringing your average share price down. Over time, besides the element of forced savings, you will hopefully see returns that you are happy with. Dollar cost averaging does not assure a profit, nor does it protect against loss in declining markets. This investment strategy requires regular investments regardless of the fluctuating price of the investment. You should consider your financial ability to continue investing through periods of low price levels.

When there is a large amount of money to invest, coming up with an investment policy and adhering to it is a must. Once an overall asset allocation mix is chosen based on your goals and objectives, stick to it and change only if there are significant changes in the economy, the portfolio, and/or your goals and objectives. Then, on a regular basis, either quarterly, semiannually, or annually, rebalance the portfolio back to the asset allocation you had started with. With this strategy, your investment mix does not get skewed towards more or less risk and volatility. Many current portfolio managers have the capability of providing this rebalancing process on an automatic basis.

A well-balanced portfolio is properly diversified by the following asset decisions:

- Growth stocks: large, medium, and small (1: see page 45)
- Value stocks: large, medium, and small
- International stocks (2): developed countries, emerging markets
- Fixed income: corporate bonds, government bonds, high yield bonds
- Real estate (3): real property, low correlation with stocks

There are many good resources to turn to that will help you take this process much further than the scope of this book. Some of those are found in chapter eleven. I think some of the best information can come from a competent and qualified financial advisor who will listen to you and develop a plan that meets your needs.

In general, a higher investment risk is best for those who:

- can accept short-term losses;
- believe gains will offset losses over the long run;
- will not leave the investment if one or two bad years occur;
- have a long "investment time horizon."

The best way to learn sound market advice is to listen to the experts. The following quotes from mutual fund leaders all stress the futility of market timing:

Peter Lynch: *"My single-most important piece of investment advice is to ignore the short-term fluctuations of the market. From one year to the next, the stock market is a coin flip. It can go up or down. The real money in stocks is made in the third, fourth and fifth year of your investments, because you are participating in a company's earnings which grow over time."*

Warren Buffet: *"I do not have, never have had, and never will have an opinion where the stock market will be a year from now."*

Sir John Templeton: *"Ignore fluctuations. Do not try to outguess the stock market. Buy a quality portfolio and invest for the long term."*

So, to drive it home, *invest for the long term and be patient!*

1 Investments in smaller company and micro-cap stocks generally carry a higher level of volatility and risk over the short term.

2. Investment risks associated with international investing, in addition to other risks, include currency fluctuations, political and economic instability and differences in accounting standards.

3. Investment risks associated with investing in the real estate fund/portfolio, in addition to other risks, include rental income fluctuation, depreciation, property tax value changes, and differences in real estate market values.

6

The Tax-Advantaged Stage

The main thrust of this stage is to try to significantly delay, reduce, and/or minimize the impact of taxes on your financial picture. Why? To accumulate and create the highest net worth you possibly can. One method of delaying the tax involves investing dollars into qualified retirement plans. This means that the dollars are made on a before tax (qualified) basis. Again, the taxes are not eliminated; they are just deferred until the funds are withdrawn. These plans include individual retirement accounts (IRAs), simplified employee pensions (SEPs), tax-sheltered annuities (TSAs), pension and profit sharing plans, 401k plans, etc.

The main advantage behind these plans is that the government has given you a significant motivation to save money because your taxable income is reduced dollar for dollar by the contribution, which will then save you anywhere from 10-35 percent of the deposit in taxes. In other words your adjusted gross income is less, which means your taxable income is reduced. While these accounts are good places to defer and delay the tax liability during your working years, they present some problems at retirement because of the tax due then. And, transferring qualified assets to heirs can present some tax nightmares if not handled carefully.

Individual retirement accounts, or IRA's have been used by taxpayers as a method of setting aside money for retirement. If you meet certain criteria, the contribution is deducted from your income and thus, lowers your tax liability. In addition, an IRA rollover account is often used for the "rollover" of qualified plans when an employee leaves an employer. We could write an entire book about IRA's alone, due to the various rules and regulations that govern their use. In general, if you are eligible for a deductible IRA contribution, we would encourage you to consider a Roth

IRA contribution because you are likely in a lower tax bracket. You'll find out more as you read the rest of this chapter.

The general principal here is to save money into these plans when you are in a higher tax bracket, and withdraw the funds at retirement when you are in a lower tax bracket. We do see some problems, though. In some cases, when a person is early in their career, and their income and tax bracket is low, it doesn't make any sense to put a lot of money into an IRA or 401k. Why defer money when you are in the lowest tax bracket you will ever be in? Instead, you may want to contribute to the 401k just up to where the employer matches those funds, but then again, only if you plan to be at that job for a few years to become vested (the employer's matching funds are yours if you are vested when you leave), and have taken care of the Security and Confidence Stage of your financial plan.

The reason the *Tax-Advantaged Stage* belongs above the *Capital Accumulation* and *Security & Confidence Stages* of the pyramid is because the money deposited into these plans is normally not available until you reach the age of 59 ½. There are methods of getting your money out early.....by borrowing the funds, or if disabled, or have a hardship situation, but for the most part money flowing into these plans should be regarded as retirement money that cannot be touched until then.

Various Types of Qualified Retirement Plans

Our intention here is not to give an in-depth description of every type of qualified plan available, but rather a brief description of each to help you understand basic terms and definitions associated with each different plan. Highlights of qualified plans include:

- Tax-deductible contributions
- Tax-deferred growth of investment earnings
- Most are protected from claims of creditors
- Available through your employer or when self employed

Some drawbacks of qualified plans include:

- Plan assets are generally illiquid until you reach age 59 ½. (10% IRS penalty applies to distributions prior to age 59 ½.).
- Annual contributions may be restricted for the successful and highly paid individual
- All distributions are taxed at ordinary income tax rates.
- Complexity of plan design, set up, and administration can be high.

Here is a brief discussion of the various retirement plans.

SIMPLE IRAs

A SIMPLE IRA is generally a good option for a business with a small number of employees. A SIMPLE IRA allows all employees to contribute a portion of their salary each paycheck, and will also require that an employer contribution be made on behalf of all eligible employees. Current guidelines allow each employee to set aside up to $12,500 ($15,000 if age 50 or over) in 2006. Contributions made to the plan will be 100 percent tax deductible. In addition, the employer must *either* match employee contributions dollar for dollar up to 3 percent of an employee's compensation *or* make a contribution of 2 percent of compensation for all eligible employees, regardless of whether they are contributing their own money to the plan. SIMPLE IRAs are easy to set up, very inexpensive to administer, and very attractive for smaller businesses looking to offer a qualified retirement plan without a lot of cost or hassle.

401k Plans

With a 401k plan, employees may choose to defer up to $15,000 ($20,000 if age 50 or over) annually into the plan on a pre-tax basis. In addition, the employer may elect to contribute a portion into the individual employee's account. For example, suppose an employee earning $60,000 of annual income contributes the full 15% into the plan and the employer makes a 3 percent matching contribution. The total contribution made into the plan would be $10,800 ($9,000 plus 3 percent of $60,000, or $1,800).

The employer may place a vesting schedule on the matching contributions. You would be required to remain with the employer a certain number of years for the matching contribution to "vest." A summary of 401k plan benefits include:

- High contribution limits for the employer and employees
- A competitive plan to attract and retain key people
- Loan provisions for hardships and emergencies
- Flexibility with respect to matching contributions

Safe Harbor 401k Plans

A safe harbor 401k plan is intended to encourage plan participation among all employees and ease the administrative burden by eliminating IRS tests normally required with a traditional 401k plan. A safe harbor 401k plan allows employees to contribute a percentage of their pay into the plan. It then **requires** an employer contribution on behalf of all eligible employees whether they are participating in the plan or not. This contribution is also always immediately vested. While there are several permitted matching formulas, one example would be: 100 percent of participant contributions up to 3 percent of pay, plus an additional 50 percent of participant contributions up to the next 2 percent of pay.

Roth 401k

A Roth 401k is a new type of retirement plan that combines the tax treatment of a Roth IRA with annual contribution limits of a traditional 401k. You may opt to take advantage of the Roth 401k if currently in a lower tax environment today than you likely will be in retirement. Such a plan allows you to contribute up to $15,000 annually on an after-tax basis. In other words, there is no tax benefit today associated with the contributions. However, the plan assets grow 100 percent tax-deferred and, provided certain requirements are met, all plan assets are withdrawn on a tax-free basis after age fifty-nine and a half.

Profit Sharing Plans

Profit sharing plans are designed to allow the employer to contribute to the plan on a discretionary basis. Depending on the terms of the plan, there is no set amount an employer needs to contribute each year. If contributions are made, you must have a set formula for determining how the contributions are allocated among all eligible plan participants. The maximum combined contribution limit the employer can deduct is 25 percent of total eligible payroll (maximum income per employee for consideration in 2006 is $220,000). The maximum amount that can be allocated to the employee's account is 100 percent of total annual pay, or $44,000 in 2006, whichever is less. There are no employee deferrals allowed without adding a 401k feature.

With a profit sharing plan, the main benefit to the business owner is the flexible nature of the contributions. It is possible to adjust contributions each year, depending on profitability of the clinic, as long as contributions are frequent and ongoing. A real, tangible benefit of a profit sharing plan for the employee is having contributions to the plan tied to the performance and overall profitability of the business.

Money Purchase Plans

A money purchase plan is very similar to a profit sharing plan in terms of contribution limits, benefits to employer and employee, setup and ongoing administrative costs, and eligibility. The primary difference is that employer contribution is a plan requirement. This amount is stated in the plan document. The benefit of a money purchase plan for the employer, is the fixed annual contributions to the plan make it easier to budget, and offers a measure of comfort and predictability for the employee. The inflexibility is often a big enough drawback that most businesses gravitate to the other choices. It is beyond the scope of this text, but for certain situations (i.e., a small number of employees with one or two older and highly paid employees), a money purchase plan and/or a variation of it can provide for sizable annual deferral limits that exceed the other plans.

Simplified Employee Pensions (SEP IRAs)

A SEP IRA is a retirement plan that looks much like a profit sharing plan. The contribution limit is 25 percent of employee compensation up to a maximum of $44,000 in 2006. The administrative costs associated with a SEP IRA are very minimal, as are reporting and tax filing requirements. The plan must cover all employees who have worked for the business in three of the past five years and are twenty-one years or older. SEP IRA plans are attractive for small businesses and professional practices that have unpredictable cash flow, as contributions to the plan can vary or not be made at all, depending on profitability. The contributions are 100 percent employer-paid with no employee contributions allowed.

SEP IRAs can also be particularly attractive for someone who has a small side business that is run from their home. Contributions for self-employment income are based on net income, minus 50 percent of self-employment taxes paid and any deductible plan contributions or a maximum of $44,000. Since self-employment income is taxed very heavily, such a plan can be a very effective tool to lessen the tax burden. In addition, SEP plans provide creditor protection at both the federal and state level.

In summary, qualified plans are an integral part of your retirement, and there are many ways in which you can design a plan. When your income is at the highest tax bracket, we generally advocate taking full advantage of the plan available to you through your employer and contributing the maximum annual contribution limit allowable under current tax law. If you have just started work and have questions or concerns regarding the existing plan or a new plan, we encourage you to contact a competent financial advisor for several reasons:

- Your qualified plan will likely be your largest retirement asset, and as such should be carefully invested and monitored.
- Tax laws surrounding such plans have changed considerably and continue to change each year. This requires more time on your part to ensure that you have the most appropriate plan that provides you maximum benefit given your circumstances.
- Tax arbitrage planning opportunities exist. You should invest in a qualified plan at a high tax bracket and withdraw the funds at a lower bracket. So, your retirement income will likely come from several sources as you design a retirement income strategy to maximize your after-tax income.

Calculating Your Tax Bracket

Just for you, we have taken the 10,000 page tax code and narrowed it down to two pages (see pages 55-56). Wouldn't that be nice if preparing our taxes was that easy! This is, of course, a basic guide only, just for education purposes, and doesn't factor in some of the specifics such as child care, student loan interest deductions, moving expenses, etc. But, surprisingly, this is fairly accurate in estimating the federal tax liability.

We encourage working with your accountant, running one of the tax software packages, or simply using this guide any time you have a major change in your life that will affect your taxes. Family changes such as a birth, death, or a marriage all affect the tax that you owe. Financial changes such as a new job, a raise, going back to school, buying or moving to a new house will also impact your tax liability, and a new calculation should be made. Compare your calculation to the amount you are having withheld from your paycheck, and if you are withholding too much, change this with your employer by filling out a new W-4 form.

This is especially useful for a student graduating in May or June and starting employment mid-year. If you don't work with your employer on the correct tax withholding, they will take out an amount that would correspond to you working for the whole year. Generally, there are many expenses and having a higher tax home pay would most likely be more beneficial than getting a tax refund the following spring.

There are some important basic points to understand about taxes. First, getting a large refund isn't really all that smart. It means that you just gave the government an interest free loan for the year. If you are a terrible saver and use this as a forced savings plan, I'm guessing it still backfires on you because you know the lump sum tax refund is coming and you have plans for spending that amount too! In any event, I suggest that you estimate your tax liability in advance and try to end up about even. That avoids any under-withholding penalties, and also any unexpected tax liability due that you may not be prepared for.

The second point is that it is always in your best interest to make more money! We've heard people say: "I just got a raise (or a bonus, or whatever)

and it jumped me into the next tax bracket, so I'm going to take home less!"
That's not how it works. The tax system is a progressive tax and the more
income you make, the more you take home. It's just that each additional
dollar is taxed at a higher percentage, but the first dollars are taxed the
same. Repeated, moving into a higher tax bracket affects the last of your
dollars you earn, but the first dollars are still taxed at the same rate.

As an example, let's look at the Basic Federal Tax Estimator on the next
page. Plug in your income (wages, interest income, etc) and subtract
contributions to pretax accounts to get your adjusted gross income. From
that, you subtract your personal exemptions and either the standard
deduction or your itemized deductions, whichever is higher. Then, look up
your tax bracket on the chart. The tax bracket is the tax on each additional
dollar you earn, or the tax that is saved by virtue of reducing your taxable
income by a dollar.

Suppose you are single and your taxable income happens to be exactly
$74,200. Your best friend's taxable income comes in at $74,201, or $1 more.
Bummer for them, right? Yes and no. Their tax liability is only 28 cents
more than yours, because each new dollar is taxed at the 28 percent rate.
They still have a take home pay of 72 cents more than you, so while at a
higher tax bracket, their take home pay is more. The total tax is calculated
as follows:

First $7,550 of taxable income:	$755 ($7,550 x .1)
Next $23,100 of taxable income	$3,465 ($23,100 x .15)
Next $43,550 of taxable income	$10,888 ($43,550 x .25)
Total Tax:	$15,108

Your friend's tax bill would be calculated the same as yours with another 28
of tax liability on the $1 above $74,200 at the 28 percent tax bracket. Work
through your own situation a few times and this should be easier to
understand.

Basic Federal Tax Estimator

(This is a guide only. This does not factor in child care, student loan interest deductions, medical expenses, moving, etc.)

Gross Income: *Wages, Interest income, etc.*

Minus: **Adjustments:** *IRA, 401(k), TSA, etc.*   -

Equals: **Adjusted Gross Income (AGI)**   =

Minus:

> **Personal Exemptions** ($3,300 x # in   -
> household)
> (Phased out as income exceeds certain limits)

And the higher of:

> **Standard Deduction** (Single: $5,150; Married: -
> $10,300)

Or

> **Itemized Deductions**
>
> - State Income Tax
>
> - Home Mortgage Interest and
>   Property Tax
>
> - Charitable Contributions

Equals: **Taxable Income**   =

_____

Federal Income Tax Due: (See Tax Table Below)

2006 Individual Income Tax Rates

Single				Married Filing Jointly			
$ -	to	7,550	10.00%	$ -	To	15,100	10.00%
7,551	to	30,650	15.00%	15,101	To	61,300	15.00%
30,651	to	74,200	25.00%	61,301	To	123,700	25.00%
74,201	to	154,800	28.00%	123,701	To	188,450	28.00%
154,801	to	336,550	33.00%	188,451	To	336,550	33.00%
336,551	-		35.00%	336,551	-		35.00%

There are substantial tax benefits with a variety of non-qualified investments also. The term non-qualified means that there is no immediate tax deduction when contributing to these accounts, but the tax benefits can be more beneficial over your lifetime. The following assets are generally part of the capital accumulation stage, but we'll provide the discussion of the tax reduction strategy of each technique in this chapter.

Stocks: As stocks appreciate in value (for this discussion, we'll assume they appreciate!) there is no tax due on the appreciation until the stock is sold. Along the way, if any dividends are paid, the tax rate is lower (15 percent for the highest tax bracket) than the ordinary income tax rate. In addition, when the stock is sold, if held for over a year, the gain is taxed at the lower 15 percent capital gain rate. So, there is a benefit of tax deferral during the holding period and tax minimizing due to the gain being treated as a capital gain.

Roth IRAs: Assuming you have all of your Security and Confidence Stage issues taken care of, and your income is such that you can use Roth IRAs, I would recommend it. You do not get a current tax deduction, but under the current law, all of the growth (again...assuming it grows!) is tax deferred. Then, when you take the money out of the Roth IRA at retirement, you receive it income tax free. Would you rather pay tax on the seeds going into the ground, or the end of the year harvest? Growth in a Roth IRA may not be withdrawn until the later of reaching age 59½ and maintaining your Roth IRA for a period of five years. Withdrawals not meeting these requirements are subject to a 10 percent early withdrawal penalty.

Real Estate: Real estate can be an excellent method of building wealth. Getting away from rent and into your first home is one obvious way. Another is leveraging the equity you have in your existing real estate into additional property. The growth is tax deferred and there are some favorable strategies available upon the sale and/or disposition. As for financing your house, contrary to popular belief, it can make sense to put little money down and stretch the mortgage out (and the tax deduction) in favor of freeing up cash flow for other goals and objectives. For a comprehensive discussion of this topic, we'd encourage you to pick up Doug Andrew's book, *Missed Fortune*.

Life Insurance: The benefits of a life insurance policy with cash values are much like those of the Roth IRA, with some additional features. As an accumulation tool, there is a cost for the insurance, so this is appropriate for someone who is younger and in good health and has a longer investment time horizon. The cash values grow tax deferred and can be accessed tax free, if structured properly. It is generally best to avoid having the policy become a Modified Endowment Policy (MEC), which happens when the premiums paid exceed the limits established for a particular age and death benefit amount. This is why it is important to work with a very knowledgeable insurance or financial professional, who is experienced with these issues.

Having a permanent life insurance policy can help you maximize your overall net worth in some other ways, too. You reduce your need for term insurance, which frees up cash. In fact, the most beneficial time to have a permanent life insurance policy in place is at retirement because of all of the advantages it provides. Briefly, you can be more aggressive in using and enjoying your other assets because the life insurance essentially provides a "permission slip" to do so. Work with your financial advisor to coordinate this with your overall financial plan.

State Sponsored 529 College Plans: There are a number of methods of putting investments in your children or grandchildren's name. If the funds are ultimately to help them with their future college education expenses, a 529 plan is the answer. Some states allow a state tax deduction on the contributions and all of the plans grow tax deferred. If the funds are withdrawn for tuition, room and board and "qualifying" education needs, the funds can be withdrawn tax free, under current tax laws. These funds can even be transferred between family members. For a lengthier discussion, read the next chapter of this book and/or go to www.savingforcollege.com. However, make sure that your own financial security is assured and your financial pyramid is sound before aggressively putting money into your children's accounts.

Annuities: An annuity is marketed by an insurance company as their answer to other investments. There are numerous benefits of non-qualified annuities as financial instrument. Namely, annuities grow tax deferred, you can switch between the separate accounts in a variable annuity without tax implications, and there are some death benefit guarantees to protect the value for your heirs. Some disadvantages include withdrawals from annuities prior to age 59½ are subject to a 10 percent early withdrawal penalty, as well as potential deferred sales charges.

What Do You Do At Retirement?

Estimating your retirement needs is an important factor to consider at this stage of the pyramid. A financial planning rule of thumb is to figure on needing 70 percent to 80 percent of your pre-retirement income, although more and more people are enjoying a retirement lifestyle that is close to their working years. This figure should be based on the income you plan to be earning at retirement, not that which you're making today. To estimate this, look at your current expenses and subtract the expenses and savings that will not be needed at retirement, and add in extra expenses (travel, medical, etc.) that may be needed then. Consider the following:

- Will you still be paying a mortgage?
- Do you anticipate hefty medical expenses for yourself or spouse?
- Do you wish to travel extensively?
- Will your day-to-day living expenses be similar, or less, than what they are now?

If your budget allows, and you have your Security and Confidence Stage taken care of, then take full advantage of any 401 (k) or similar plans your employer offers, at least up until the amount that the employer matches. This type of retirement investment defers tax payment on the contributed earnings until the money is withdrawn, usually at retirement. If your employer matches any of your contribution, this is an added tax benefit.

If you are self-employed, then consider a Simplified Employee Pension (SEP) or SIMPLE retirement plan, which also allows you to take advantage of the pre-tax growth that has been described in this chapter. Deciding on the correct retirement plan will be something that a competent financial advisor can help you with.

Universal Retirement Truths

Over the years, as retirement planning has become increasingly complicated, there are four simple "truths" behind any advice we offer on retirement planning, no matter how complicated the specific issue.

Start Early

The sooner you begin contributing to your retirement plan, the more time your money has to compound. You can always make adjustments to keep your investment allocation on track with your risk tolerance and time horizon profile. However, if you delay getting started entirely, it is very difficult to catch up.

Diversify

With regard to your retirement plan, after you have determined an appropriate investment allocation for your contributions, make sure you understand the investment objectives of each individual fund you are investing in.

Two funds with different names may have very similar investment objectives as well as holdings. Deferring into each fund will not give you the same degree of diversification as investing in two funds with different objectives.

We recommend you work with a financial professional to determine an appropriate asset allocation for your retirement assets and make sure you achieve a high level of diversification among the investment options.

Invest Consistently

Most plans allow for contributions to be made on a payroll deduction basis. This allows for contributions to be made to your investments each and every month. This eliminates any tendency to "time" the market and put larger contributions at the optimal share price. Regular investing over time is a proven method that "forces" you to buy more shares when the price of a fund is down and fewer when prices are higher.

Dollar cost averaging will produce a lower average cost per share over time.

Hang Tough

If your retirement is still fifteen, twenty, even thirty years away, it is appropriate (even crucial) to construct a more aggressive investment allocation than that of an investment objective with a shorter time horizon. It is perfectly natural that such an investment allocation will experience higher levels of short-term fluctuation. This is necessary to potentially achieve a higher long-term rate of return.

As the time when you will begin drawing on this money draws nearer, it will be necessary to begin shifting a greater percentage of your assets towards investments geared more towards capital preservation. The time to worry about this is not during your peak earning years when retirement is still many years away. Ideally, at retirement, you have multiple income sources and are withdrawing money from your qualified plans to "fill up" your 25 percent bracket and supplementing that with withdrawals from your non-qualified funds and variable life policies for maximum tax leverage and efficiency. This is an area where the advice and wisdom of an experienced financial planner will be very valuable.

7

529 College Savings Plans

When it comes to planning for your children's future education costs, the 529 College Savings Plans are one of the most important accounts to consider. From an investment standpoint, such plans enjoy tax-deferred growth of earnings, extremely generous contribution limits, and currently tax-free distributions of investment gains for all qualified education expenses. (We'll expand on qualified expenses in a moment.)

Our opinion is that the features that make such plans so attractive have less to do with their tax treatment and more to do with issues of control and flexibility.

Let's look at these plans from two difference perspectives:

- Investment and tax features
- Control and flexibility features

Tax and Investment Features

One frustrating aspect of investment planning from a tax perspective is that, when income increases beyond certain annual amounts, many investments that have attractive tax treatment become unavailable (Roth IRAs) or annual contribution limits become more restrictive as income goes up (401k plans). Neither of these is an issue with the 529 Plan. All investment earnings on the plan grow 100 percent tax-deferred, and the contribution limits are such that they would rarely be restrictive for the purpose of funding a child's education.

Contributions

Contributions to 529 plans are not federally* tax-deductible but are considered gifts for federal and estate tax purposes. Anyone may take advantage of the annual gift tax exclusion by contributing $12,000 per year ($24,000 for married couples) to any beneficiary. For financially independent taxpayers, there is a very unique rule for 529 Plans that allows for an individual to utilize five years worth of annual gift tax exclusion by contributing up to $60,000 ($120,000 for married couples) in one calendar year.

The limits imposed on 529 Plans are, generally speaking, so high that it is difficult to envision a scenario where it would become restrictive. The total limits outside of the above discussed annual limits do vary a bit from state to state. They are in the neighborhood of $250,000 to $290,000 per beneficiary! Provided you get started early on planning for your children or grandchildren's future education costs to take full advantage of the tax-deferred growth of investment earnings, such limits should not present a problem.

*It should be noted that with many state plans there is a tax deduction for contributions to the state plan where you hold your primary residence. Because each state varies and the laws are changing, consult with a financial advisor who is familiar with the rules in your state.

Distributions

Suppose that money has been contributed to a 529 Plan for the benefit of a child or grandchild, and the plan balance has grown significantly over the years. Now it is time to begin withdrawing the money to pay for college expenses, so what happens? When money is withdrawn from the account, it will be considered one of two things: a qualified distribution or a non-qualified distribution.

- Distributions that are utilized to pay for qualified expenses such as room, board, tuition, and certain expenses will be considered qualified withdrawals, and as such are free of both federal and, currently, state income tax. For the parent with a long time horizon and children bound for academic greatness (and the accompanying price tag), there is potential to build up and withdraw all investment gains free of tax!

- Distributions that are utilized for anything other than a qualified expense will be considered a non-qualified distribution. The investment earnings will be taxed as ordinary income for the beneficiary and subject to a 10 percent penalty.

Control and Flexibility Features

The tax and investment features of IRC Section 529 College Plans are undeniably attractive and make such plans a very powerful financial tool for the high-income medical specialist. However, given the uncertainty of a young child's academic future, we often find reluctance among our clients to fund such vehicles for your child, who may or may not need the money. These uncertainties are very well addressed in 529 plans.

Let's look at some of their benefits from a control and flexibility standpoint.

Who controls the account? The account owner controls the account. If your child reaches the age of majority in your home state, the 529 Plan balance does not become an asset of your child! You, as account owner, control how and when distributions are to be made.

Who can contribute to the account? Anyone may make contributions to the plan.

What happens if my child receives a scholarship or goes to a less expensive school? Perhaps one of the most attractive features of 529 Plans from a flexibility standpoint is the ability to change beneficiaries at any point. However, in order to avoid triggering penalty on investment earnings, the new beneficiary must be a family member of the previous beneficiary. The ability to move money in one designated 529 Plan to another child's plan, should he or she not go to school, attend a less expensive school, receive a scholarship, or any other reason, is a unique feature that gives parents a great deal of flexibility. Specifically, if the plan beneficiary does receive a scholarship, an exception allows the student to withdraw money from the 529 Plan without a penalty.

What happens if money is not used for college? If the money being withdrawn from a 529 Plan is being used for anything other than a qualified higher education expense, the investment earnings will be taxed at the beneficiaries' tax rate, plus a 10 percent penalty on earnings. Pulling money out of 529 Plans for non-qualified expenses should be avoided. However, as the earnings are taxed at the beneficiary's rate, it is not too terrible as the account has grown completely tax-deferred!

Must the beneficiary go to school in the state whose plan I used? No. Currently, all states recognize other state-sponsored 529 Plans, and as such, all distributions for qualified expenses will be both federally and state tax-exempt.

Funding Your Child's IRC Section 529 College Savings Plan

With all the advantages of 529 Plans, the obvious question becomes, "How do we fund a plan for our child?"

When determining how to take full advantage of such plans, there are several assumptions you can predict with a fairly high degree of accuracy. Such factors include:

- Year in which your child enters college
- How many years (four or five) of post-secondary education you wish to be able to fund
- The *average* inflation-adjusted cost for both public and private education costs
- The percentage of the total cost you as a parent wish to be able to pay for

There are also many more variables you must simply make a best estimate for. A few of these factors include:

- The rate of inflation for college costs. College costs have experienced significant levels of increase over the years and will likely continue to rise at a greater rate than the overall cost of living.
- The investment rate of return of the assets in the 529 Plan.
- Where your child will attend school

All of these variables must be considered when determining how to fund your child's plan to arrive at the most important objective: having adequate funds available within the plan to be able to pay for the type of education, the length of education, and the location of the education you planned for. Any outcome other than this will result in one of two scenarios:

- Not enough money saved up in the 529 Plan. This will likely result in funds being withdrawn from other investment vehicles that have not grown tax-deferred and will likely not enjoy the tax benefits when withdrawn. As qualified distributions will be both state and federally tax-exempt, investment gains from other sources will likely be subject to tax! As discussed earlier, this is where an over-funded variable life insurance policy can come in very handy.

- Too much money saved up in the 529 Plan. The likely result of too much money in the plan will be excessive non-qualified distributions. While the earnings will be taxed at your child's rate and thus at a lower rate, this is only in the event that it is withdrawn for the benefit of the beneficiary. Should the money *not* be withdrawn for the benefit of your child, all investment earnings will taxed at *your* ordinary income rate plus a 10 percent penalty! So, err on the conservative side and fund a 529 Plan at a level you feel comfortable with.

Our conclusion is that 529 College Savings Plans are excellent financial tools for the purpose of saving for future college costs. Like all aspects of your financial planning, regular monitoring is critical. As your child's academic greatness (hopefully!) begins to materialize, adjusting the contributions to the plan accordingly will ensure that the many benefits can be maximized.

The tax laws that created the 529 plans were introduced with a variety of estate planning laws that actually had a "sunset provision" in 2010. This means that if the laws are not reviewed and extended, the 529 plans as discussed above would be limited or discontinued, meaning the appreciation in these accounts might be taxed at distribution. So...stay tuned. The general assumption being made now is that these plans have been so popular that the laws will change to extend the benefits for many years to come.

8

Estate Planning with Asset Protection Strategies

Asset protection planning should not be viewed as a strategy to avoid paying legitimate and reasonable creditors, but as a process to protect your personal assets from unreasonable creditors. *"Unreasonable Creditors"* are those who bring frivolous lawsuits or get unreasonable jury awards related to medical malpractice or personal liability claims such as automobile or slip and fall accidents. These unreasonable creditors do exist. They are the predators looking to sue anyone who is successful. It could be any legal action where a valid claim simply doesn't exist.

In general, "asset protection" is about putting up barriers in front of the unreasonable creditors to make it difficult or impossible for them to get your personal and business assets. The key questions are:

1. What should I do?
2. When should I do it?
3. How far do I need to go?

What Should I Do?

The first step in navigating through the asset protection choices is to get educated. This chapter is not intended to be an exhaustive treatise on asset protection, but a primer to get you going in the right direction. It also is not intended to be legal advice and should not be taken as such; it is for information purposes only. Before implementing any asset protection strategy, you should consult with an attorney licensed to practice law in your state.

Exempt Assets

The first line of defense against unreasonable creditors is the protection you get from the state you live in. Each state, through its statutes, exempts certain assets from creditors. These assets can include all or a portion of the following:

- *Home:* In many states, you get an exemption from creditors for your home. This, however, is usually not an unlimited exemption, and in some states (New Jersey, for example) there is no exemption at all. Other states (such as Florida) give an unlimited exemption, meaning a creditor cannot force you to sell your home to pay off a judgment no matter what the value is. While these two states present both ends of the spectrum, the bulk of the states fall somewhere in between. An example is Minnesota, where the statute allows you to protect $200,000 of equity in your home. If the difference between your home's market value and all mortgages is greater than $200,000, a creditor can force you to sell your home, paying to the creditor any amount over the exemption.

- *Life insurance:* Some states will protect life insurance partially or entirely. This can be both the cash value and/or death benefit.
    - States such as Texas protect all of the cash value paid into a life insurance contract. This means a creditor cannot force you to withdraw funds to pay off a debt.
    - To contrast the laws of Texas, Minnesota only protects death benefits of $20,000 if paid to the surviving spouse or child and cash value of $4,000. Any amount above these can be reached by a creditor. Check with your local attorney in the event this has changed.

- *Annuities:* Annuities are similar to life insurance. Each state decides how much, if any, can be protected from creditors.

- *Individual retirement accounts:* IRAs are also given a certain amount of protection by state laws, and the protection varies from state to state. Again, it can be all, nothing, or somewhere in between. The trend, however, is for greater protection to be given to these types of accounts. You should be aware that these laws are changing. In fact, Congress recently passed new bankruptcy legislation that included provisions for increased protection of Traditional and Roth IRA's owned by a person in a bankruptcy proceeding.

- *ERISA-governed retirement plans:* These plans are most commonly employer-sponsored profit sharing/401k plans. They are different from IRAs in that they are governed by federal law instead of state law. In most cases, federal law will trump state laws, including judgments that require an ERISA-governed plan to liquidate assets to pay a creditor.

An attorney licensed in your state should be contacted in order to determine what protections your state will give you against the unreasonable creditor.

Basic Estate Planning: Wills or Revocable Trusts

The foundation for any asset protection strategy is to have your basic estate plan in place. The two primary documents you can choose from for your basic estate plan are the Will or the Revocable Living Trust. While neither of these estate planning documents give much asset protection during your life, they can (if properly drafted) give good protection to your heirs.

The Will

Having a Will does not avoid probate; it is an instruction manual to the probate court on how your probate-eligible property should be distributed, who should do it, and, if your children are under the age of majority, who should be their guardian. While you are alive, it does nothing to give you asset protection as you continue to own your property in your name. It may give some asset protection to your heirs, depending on the complexity of the planning.

The probate process is designed to be a creditor's forum. Any known creditors must be given notice, and there is a waiting period for creditors to stake their claim.

The Revocable Living Trust

A revocable living trust is an alternative to using a Will for your primary estate planning documents. Having a properly funded revocable living trust will avoid probate. While it will avoid the probate process, it does not protect your assets from creditors. It can, however, if correctly drafted, give good asset protection for your heirs after your death.

The fact that the revocable living trust, if properly and completely funded, avoids the probate process and the creditor-friendly rules that come with it is reason enough to choose them over Wills for your basic estate planning vehicles.

Family Limited Liability Companies and Family Limited Partnerships

One of the more common strategies used in asset protection to build upon the basic estate planning is the (family) limited liability company (FLLC) or (family) limited partnership (FLP).

FLLC

A limited liability company is a new form of business entity that has become increasingly popular. It combines the liability protection of a corporation with the tax and asset protection advantages of a general partnership. All fifty states have enacted LLC laws, with most of them looking and feeling like a general partnership. Some states (Minnesota, in particular) have taken on the feel of the corporation with the two levels of management (governor and manager). This feature makes it ideal for the family LLC, because it allows husband and wife to maintain various levels of control over the company depending on their life circumstances.

An LLC can elect to be taxed like a corporation or a partnership. However, the majority of LLCs today elect to be taxed like a partnership. That means these LLCs do not pay income tax. The income flows through directly to the members and is reported on their personal tax returns.

To begin the LLC, articles of organization are filed with the state in which you intend to set up the company. Some states (such as Minnesota) allow you to keep the names of the members, governors, and managers private with only the name of the organizer being filed (in most cases, the attorney that sets up the company). Having this anonymity can provide for benefits and is an important component of an asset protection strategy.

FLP

General Partnerships

A general partnership is formed when two or more persons agree to carry on a business together to make a profit. It is as simple as that, and no writing has to be made and no documents need to be filed with the state except for registering the name to be used. It is good practice, however, for any partnership to have a written partnership agreement so all partners understand their rights and responsibilities. The problem with a general partnership is that all partners are jointly and separately liable for all debts of the partnership. The general partnership should be avoided at all costs because of this liability trap. If a partnership is to be used in an asset protection setting, it should be formed as a limited partnership.

Limited Partnerships

A limited partnership consists of one or more general partners and one or more limited partners. A general partner handles the control and management of the partnership. The tradeoff for this is that he or she has unlimited personal liability for all debts and obligations of the partnership. The limited partners cannot be involved in the control or management of the partnership, but they do enjoy protection from the debts of the partnership because their liability is limited to their investments in the entity. If a limited partner does participate in the control or management of the partnership, they may lose their limited liability.

Choosing Between the Two

For many years, the FLP was the entity of choice for asset protection and the minimization of estate taxes, but since its advent, the LLC is fast becoming the entity of choice because it is more flexible than the FLP and because there is no unlimited liability for the general partners as there is with a FLP. In a family LLC, the husband and wife can be involved in the management of the company without losing their liability shield while there are no creditors. If a lawsuit arises, the spouse/defendant resigns from their management role but retains their personal liability protection.

Creditor Cannot Reach Assets of a FLP or FLLC

In most states, the only remedy for a judgment creditor of an LLC or a limited partnership is a "charging order." A charging order is a legal remedy that gives the creditor the right to receive any distributions from an FLP or FLLC. It does not give the creditor the right to become an owner or the right to have a say in the management of the company. The creditor only receives the distributions intended to go to the owner/debtor. If this happens, the FLP/FLLC will simply choose not to make any distributions. The poison pill, however, is that even if the FLP/FLLC does not make a distribution, the creditor is responsible for the tax consequences as if a distribution had been made when the entity is taxed as a partnership.

The idea behind charging order protection is simple enough: Owners should not be involuntarily forced into a partnership with somebody they do not choose. To get complete protection from this strategy, however, great care must be put into the "operating agreement" to give the maximum protection possible from creditors. Using this entity to hold the assets you most want to protect allows you to protect them from creditors.

Trusts

Irrevocable Trusts

In planning, it is important to keep the revocable living trust concept talked about separate from the irrevocable trust. The revocable living trust can be amended or revoked (you retain complete control as long as you are alive and competent), but it gives limited asset protection. On the other hand, the irrevocable trust will protect your assets (assuming the transfer of property was not a fraudulent conveyance), but you lose all control and benefit. In a properly executed asset protection strategy, they do play an important role.

One of the more common uses is to own life insurance. If the trust is created properly and all of the administrative formalities are followed, it will keep the proceeds out of a deceased person's estate for tax purposes and keep them away from creditors.

Asset Protection Trusts

A strategy that is gaining popularity is the asset protection trust (APT). An APT is a self-settled trust, meaning it is funded by the creator of the trust, who is also the beneficiary. This is different from the irrevocable trust discussed above, because in a traditional irrevocable trust, the intended beneficiary is usually the spouse or children and not the person who creates the trust.

There are two main types of APTs: the domestic APT and the offshore (foreign) APT.

Domestic APT

In many states, the self-settled APT is not allowed. But in a minority of states, recent legislation is beginning to allow such asset protection vehicles. Eight states, (Alaska, Delaware, Rhode Island, Missouri, Utah, Oklahoma, South Dakota, and Nevada) now allow some form of a self-settled trust to be set up that is outside the reach of creditors. These are very new and have yet to be challenged in court. Many legal scholars believe they are unconstitutional because of the "Full Faith and Credit" clause of the constitution, which says, "A state is to recognize the judgment from another state." This sets up a conflict of state laws issue (the self-settled APT is exempt from judgment creditors in the state it was created) and the United States Constitution. This means the creditor must simply register the judgment and does not have to initiate the lawsuit all over again in that state.

Until the above mentioned conflict of laws issue is settled in court, the domestic APT should probably be avoided unless you happen to live in one of the states where they are recognized. These trusts are usually expensive to set up and administer, and they are probably not a good choice for asset protection unless you are a citizen of a state that has enacted the legislation.

Offshore APT

An offshore or foreign APT is similar to the domestic APT except the trust situs (location) is in a foreign jurisdiction. The Cook Islands or Nevis are two popular destinations. These trusts are self-settled, but the trustee is located in one of these foreign jurisdictions, thereby putting them out of reach of the United States courts. A creditor would not simply be able to register a United States judgment in one of these jurisdictions; they would have to initiate a new lawsuit.

While the trustee and trust may be outside the reach of the United States courts, the creator of the trust is not unless he or she leaves the country. Many state and federal judges despise this setup and will do whatever is in their power to unwind this type of trust, including putting the creator of the trust in jail for contempt of court. There is a long line of cases that deal with this issue, many not favorable to the debtor. These trusts are also very expensive to set up and administer and should probably only be used in extreme cases and not with all assets. Consult with an expert asset protection attorney before considering these trusts.

When Should I Do It?

Time should be used as an ally. Having a plan in place and implemented for a period of time before an event (judgment or death) occurs will give the plan a better chance of withstanding an attack by a creditor or the Internal Revenue Service. If you wait until a lawsuit is initiated or even after an event occurs that may cause a lawsuit to be initiated, it may be too late because any transfer may be deemed a "fraudulent conveyance" and will likely quash any asset protection strategies you implement, on the theory that their only purpose was to deny creditors their claims.

How Far Do I Need to Go?

You need to take the steps necessary to give you and your family "peace of mind." Assess your risk with the cost of implementing an asset protection plan and take the action that gives you the protection you're comfortable with. With that in mind, here are some planning rules of thumb.

Planning Rules of Thumb

The following rules of thumb are a guide to assist you in deciding if you need asset protection planning. However, the final decisions must weigh the risk of a lawsuit with the cost of the protection. In many cases, the tools referenced in this chapter make good sense for successful individuals, no matter the stage of his or her career.

1. *If you do not have children:* You may not need to undertake any estate planning at this time, but you should consult with an attorney in your area to make the final decision.

2. *If you have children:* You need to take some action to get the bare minimum for estate planning. You should be considering guardians for custody of your children and trustees to handle their finances if both parents die. If asset protection concerns or will concern you, you should begin with revocable trusts. Another option is to use testamentary trusts inside of your Will. Keep in mind these techniques alone do not provide asset protection for you though they can provide protection to your heirs. These options are more expensive than basic wills, but it will be money well spent as these will be the foundation of your overall plan.

3. *Early in your career:* If you are just starting out, you most likely will have a low net worth and high debt load. Even though your net worth is relatively low, you should consider enlisting an attorney to help you decide whether wills or revocable trusts with pour over Wills are appropriate for your main estate planning tools.

4. *Business Owner or Professional Practice:* If you have developed a successful business or professional practice and asset protection concerns you, you should look to implementing the following procedures if your state-given exemptions do not give you the protection you want and need:

    a.   If you have substantial after-tax investments, including cash value life insurance, annuities, rental real estate or recreational property, you should consider a family limited liability company.

    b.   If you have a family LLC, use it for your cash value life insurance. Then you could use a separate Irrevocable Life Insurance Trust for your term insurance with total death benefits greater than $1.5 million to avoid estate taxes and protect the death benefits for your heirs.

Conclusion

If the intended goal of asset protection is to be completely judgment-proof, successful asset protection becomes extremely difficult. However, if the goal is to protect a portion of your estate against the unreasonable creditor, that goal can be obtained with the help of an experienced financial planner and attorney. Without successful asset protection planning, you will lose all assets that are not exempt if you get a judgment awarded against you. With the right planning, you will be able to build walls between you and your creditors that will improve your bargaining position and help you protect what you have worked so hard to earn.

Remember, you need to take action before there are any potential lawsuits against you. Otherwise, any actions taken may be unraveled by the courts.

As with every aspect of a financial plan, the estate planning and asset protection components are extensive and need to be coordinated by a professional advisor. The advisor should obviously be very knowledgeable, but also one who listens to you and your goals, and then communicates your options...so you can work together.

Disclaimers and Other Documents

The U.S. Treasury Department requires us to advise you that to the extent that this message or any attachment concerns tax matters it is not intended or written by our firm to be used, and cannot be used by any taxpayer, for the purpose of avoiding any penalties that may be imposed under the Internal Revenue Code or any other law.

What is IRS Circular 230?

The Treasury Department and the Internal Revenue Service have been engaged in an effort to curb abusive tax shelters. As part of this effort, they have issued final regulations under IRS Circular 230 "...to restore, promote, and maintain the public's confidence in those individuals and firms..." who act as tax advisors.

This is an explanation of how our correspondence with you (including e-mails) will be affected by new IRS regulations governing tax practitioners. The new rules in effect require us to add certain standard language to many of our letters, memos, e-mails, and other correspondence concerning federal tax matters. You have probably already seen similar language on written communications from your other correspondence. Although the specific wording may vary depending on the circumstances, you can expect to see notices similar to the following:

IRS Circular 230 Notice:

To the extent that this message or any attachment concerns tax matters it is not intended or written by our firm to be used, and cannot be used by any taxpayer, for the purpose of avoiding any penalties that may be imposed under the Internal Revenue Code or any other law.

The new rules require such notices to be "prominently disclosed," i.e., "readily apparent" to the reader. The notice must be in a separate section (but not in a footnote) of the correspondence. Also, "fine-print" notices won't work. The typeface used must be at least the same size as the typeface used in any discussion of facts or law.

A practitioner who fails to satisfy the requirement of the new rules risks censure, disbarment, and substantial penalties.

Please be assured that this new policy does not reflect any decrease in the quality of our services or the amount of thought we put into our correspondence with you.

9

The Speculation Stage

The speculation stage involves risking money that you can afford to lose. Some people are never comfortable with this and thus should not consider it. These people should simply build their financial pyramid wider. This stage can involve different things for different people. It might mean investing into a small business that you're starting or investing in a friend's business. It could be buying very speculative individual stocks or aggressive specialty mutual funds.

Subjecting your money where the principal has a high degree of volatility and risk has potentially high returns, but your money could also be lost completely. It is appropriate that this stage fits at the top of the pyramid because if the money is lost, it won't be devastating to your overall financial plan.

Our rule of thumb when deciding how much to risk in a business opportunity or other aggressive venture is one year's worth of net worth growth. Never invest more than this! In a worst case scenario, if you lost the entire amount of your investment, you have basically lost one year's worth of financial progress. While not fun, it is not financially devastating. People get into trouble and can't recover financially when they take a lifetime's worth of savings and gamble with it.

For a simple example, let's say that your net worth is $100,000, and conservatively projected a year from now, it will be $110,000. This growth could be from additional savings, reducing debts, and/or growth from your existing assets. In any event, the $10,000 projected growth is the amount that could be considered for a very speculative investment.

In the event that an opportunity has come along that requires more than this amount, do not be tempted to risk more. Consider lowering your investment, delaying the timing until your net worth has grown, or involving a financial partner. The following ideas are just a few examples of possibilities that exist:

- Buying individual stocks of new companies
- Buying stock in initial public offerings (IPOs)
- Buying stock on margin (Be very careful!)
- Investing in a friend's or family member's new business
- Buying raw land and/or real estate for speculation
- Trading commodities (Be careful here!)

Again, keep in mind, speculative investments, while valid financial tools, are typically used only by extremely savvy investors, and/or high net worth investors and institutions. They are not recommended to anyone who cannot afford to lose a substantial amount of their net worth. These investments carry an extraordinary amount of risk, and generally require intensive research and knowledge to carry out the investment.

In summary, no one has ever gotten into trouble financially by being too conservative for too long. Sure, there are some potential lost opportunity costs, but you can get into a lot of financial trouble by being too aggressive with too much money. That's why the financial pyramid is such a useful tool to help organize and prioritize these decisions.

10

Case Studies

Observations and Overview:

In this chapter, we provide six specific case studies that demonstrate the concepts outlined in this book. We have provided a wide variety of examples in order to show that the pyramid of financial needs can be used in most circumstances as a method of organizing and prioritizing financial decisions. Hopefully, you can relate to one of these case studies and start applying the strategies to your situation. Of course, much of this is subjective and ultimately, the correct answer merges the quantitative and qualitative aspects of the decision into a financial plan that you are comfortable with. We hope that you find the following case studies to be a very helpful addition to the understanding of the techniques presented earlier in this book.

Case Study #1: The Young Single Professional

Melissa graduated last year with a teaching degree. She plans on continuing to take courses ultimately to earn her Masters degree. This will move her up the pay range, and possibly get into administration.

She has many financial goals at this time including:

- moving from renting into her own home or condo
- continue to pay off her debts
- start a basic investment plan
- have a plan for emergencies, and unexpected events

The Numbers:

Melissa is currently making $34,000/year with an extra $1,200 for coaching the girls' golf team. She and her college roommate share an apartment so her bills are very reasonable. Fortunately, she lives very frugally and her take home pay of $2,150 allows her to pay all of her bills and still have about $8-900/month left over.

Her Net Worth Statement:

Fixed Assets:

Savings Account:	$7,000
Checking Account:	$1,000
Money Market Account:	$0
Total Fixed Assets:	<u>$8,000</u>

Variable Assets:

Roth IRA:	$0
Mutual Funds:	$500
403(b) balance:	$800
Total Variable Assets:	<u>$1,300</u>

Personal and Other Assets:

Home:	$0
Vehicle:	$8,000
Personal Property:	$5,000
Total:	<u>$13,000</u>

Total Assets:	<u>$22,300</u>

Liabilities:

Mortgage: (30 year @ 6%)	$0
Vehicle Loan: (9%)	$7,500
Credit Cards: (18%)	$2,000
Student Loans: (3.5%)	$14,000
Total Liabilities:	<u>$23,500</u>

Net Worth: (Assets minus Liabilities)	<u>-$1,200</u>

The Financial Plan:

Security and Confidence Stage:
- Set up a money market mutual fund as her emergency reserve instead of the savings account. Except for the small savings into the capital accumulation stage and the Roth IRA, continue to build up the emergency reserves so that she has a down payment ready for a home or condo in 12-24 months
- Immediately pay off the credit cards
- Secure a private individual disability policy to insure her greatest asset…..her ability to earn an income

Capital Accumulation Stage:
- Start a monthly savings program that includes putting $100/month into a mutual fund and $50/month into a variable life insurance policy to lock in her insurability and lock in the rates when younger as she anticipates getting married and starting a family some day
- Consider buying a condo next year in the $130,000 range and ideally, rent a room to a roommate to help defray some of the costs.

Tax Advantaged Stage:
- Continue the contribution into the 403(b) plan (up to the employer match), making sure that this is actively managed using a carefully constructed portfolio.
- Start contributing into a new ROTH IRA with $300/month

Speculation Stage:
- Wait until the base of the pyramid is more established

Summary:

By living frugally, and working hard to save and build her net worth, Melissa is just one month away from becoming "worthless." (Her assets will equal her liabilities.) This is a significant milestone for someone who is just getting started in her profession. Melissa is a saver, and is working hard to pay off her car loan, build savings for a potential down payment on a starter home or condo, as well as initiate other important investments. She also is happy that the financial plan addressed the very important issues of life and disability insurance as this is something that she hadn't even thought about before, but recognizes as a critical part of her overall financial plan.

Submitted by Todd D. Bramson, CFP®, ChFC, CLU

Case Study #2: The 35-Year-Old Physician Couple

Circumstances: Jennifer finished her residency five years ago and has been working hard to pay off debt, get established in her practice, while balancing time with her family. Her husband Robert, a pharmacist by training, has been home full time with their two children, ages four and one. The plan is for him to go back to work part time when the youngest is in school.

They have many financial goals at this time including:

- building "the house of their dreams" in a few years
- continuing to pay off their debts
- starting to save for their children's education
- saving for retirement
- reducing tax liability
- wealth protection
- have a plan for emergencies, and unexpected events

The Numbers:

Jennifer works at a large teaching hospital as a radiation oncologist with an annual income of $350,000. She has access to the standard employee benefit package that includes health insurance, disability insurance of 60% of income capped at $10,000/month, life insurance of one times salary, and the ability to contribute to a tax sheltered annuity, etc. Their monthly take home pay is $20,000, and their monthly expenses are $12,000, leaving $8,000/month in excess funds with which to plan.

Their Net Worth Statement:

Fixed Assets:

Savings Account:	$15,000
Checking Account:	$3,000
Certificate of Deposit:	$2,000
Total Fixed Assets:	$20,000

Variable Assets:

IRA:	$13,000
Roth IRA:	$9,000
Mutual Funds:	$10,000
Individual Stocks:	$2,000
Variable Life Cash Value:	$4,000
401k balance:	$40,000
Total Variable Assets:	$78,000

Personal and Other Assets:

Home:	$375,000
Vehicle:	$20,000
Personal Property:	$30,000
Total:	$425,000

Total Assets: $523,000

Liabilities:

Mortgage: (30 year @ 6%)	$290,000
Home Equity Line: (7%)	$15,000
Vehicle Loan: (9%)	$10,000
Credit Cards: (18%)	$2,000
Student Loans: (3.5%)	$110,000
Total Liabilities:	$427,000

Net Worth: (Assets minus Liabilities) $96,000

The Financial Plan:

Security and Confidence Stage:
- Increase umbrella liability insurance to 3 million
- Secure a personal disability policy on Jennifer to supplement the group coverage
- Increase the home equity line of credit to be used for emergencies, including paying off the car so the interest is less and tax deductible (Pay $2,000/month toward this, save the extra when paid off, to be used for the new house)
- Secure life insurance using a combination of over-funded variable adjustable policies and term insurance
- Pay off the credit cards immediately, and continue to stretch out the mortgage and student loans for the length of the loan
- Draft wills, trusts, and appropriate estate planning documents

Capital Accumulation Stage:
- Commit to saving $6,000 into the following:
- Initiate 529 plans for children's college and fund
- Initiate a fee based brokerage account to start building a portfolio of non-qualified mutual funds
- Fund variable life policies just up to the limits allowed, that don't turn the policies into modified endowment contracts
- Consider building their dream house sooner than later, to take advantage of today's lower interest rates, low down payment needed, appreciation of higher value property and allow enjoyment of the house with the family for more years

Tax Advantaged Stage:
- Continue to maximize the contribution into the 403(b) retirement plan ($15,000/year), making sure that this is actively managed using a carefully constructed portfolio

Speculation Stage:
- Wait until the base of the pyramid is more established

Summary:

Their new plan takes care of "building a moat" around the financial castle that they are starting to build. They feel more confident now that they have wills and appropriate levels of insurance. The life insurance plays an important role in the security and confidence stage as well as the capital accumulation stage and was an excellent addition to the overall financial plan. With the risk management in order, they can aggressively begin a monthly savings plan for college and mid-long term financial security. In addition, they are starting to work with an architect to build their dream home, and can pursue that sooner than they imagined. They finally feel like the "lean" years of medical school and residency are starting to pay off.

Submitted by Jesse T. Karich

Case Study #3: The Dual Income Professional Couple

Circumstances: Jim opened his dental practice 28 years ago, and Kathy recently finished pharmacy school after being a stay at home mom for over ten years. Over the past several years, a large portion of their disposable income has been allocated towards college expenses for their three children. During that time, most of their retirement savings have been cut back to a minimal level. Their youngest son will graduate from high school this year and begin college in the fall, while their oldest kids are already in college. Jim and Kathy have several financial priorities they want to address in the immediate and short-term future before they enter into retirement.

- Maintaining the college funding for all three children
- Getting their plan back on track for retirement
- Structuring a savings plan that will allow them to maximize tax efficiency and tax deductions in their working years
- Coordinating a plan that will allow them to spend and enjoy their nest egg without fear of running out of money
- Constructing an asset protection strategy to safeguard against potential lawsuits and unexpected events

The Numbers:

Jim has been a longtime owner of a small town dental practice, and Kathy recently graduated from pharmacy school and is working in a hospital. Their household income fluctuates between $250,000 and $350,000 depending on the revenue of the dental practice. Jim's business provides a group health insurance plan. His practice has sustained a group profit sharing plan that has been contributing seven percent of the employees' and his own salary at the end of every year. They have $10,000 per month after their monthly expenses to save for accomplishing their objectives.

Their Net Worth Statement:

Fixed Assets:

Savings Account:	$10,000
Money Market:	$35,000
Checking Account:	$1,000
Total Fixed Assets:	$46,000

Variable Assets:

IRA:	$56,000
Profit Sharing:	$713,000
Mutual Funds:	$200,000
Individual Stocks:	$317,000
Bonds:	$155,000
Variable Life Cash Value:	$4,000
Total Variable Assets:	$1,445,000

Personal and Other Assets:

Home:	$110,000
Vehicle:	$20,000
Rental Properties:	$120,000
Office Building:	$550,000
Total:	$800,000

Total Assets:	$2,291,000

Liabilities:

Mortgage:	$0
Credit Cards: (Paid off monthly)	$0
Total Liabilities:	$0

Net Worth (Assets minus Liabilities):	$2,291,000

The Financial Plan:

Security and Confidence Stage:
- Purchase an umbrella liability insurance of $3 million.
- Open an LLC for the rental properties.
- Continue to maintain private disability coverage.
- Secure life insurance using a combination of over-funded variable adjustable policies and term insurance.
- Draft wills, trusts, and appropriate estate planning documents.
- Work with an attorney to structure an entity-form of ownership for the practice, such as a corporation of LLC. The business is currently a sole-proprietorship. In the event a lawsuit is filed against their dental practice, creditors could potentially sue for their personal assets (stocks, bonds, etc).

Capital Accumulation Stage:
- Since the children are older and won't benefit much from the tax deferred compounding in a 529 plan, they should gift the low basis stock each year to the two older kids and have them sell it at their lower capital gains bracket (which could be 5% if they are in the 10-15% bracket and 0% in 2008).
- Use any cash and/or high basis stock to fund a 529 plan for their youngest child and use up to five years' worth of gift tax exclusions ($60,000) so that college is mostly funded at once.
- Initiate a fee-based brokerage account to start managing the mutual funds, stocks, and bonds.
- Heavily fund variable life policies, but keep them within the limits allowed by the IRS so that they don't turn into modified endowment contracts. This provides another opportunity for tax-favored growth for retirement, while also addressing their life insurance needs.

Tax Advantaged Stage:
- Restructure company retirement plan from a profit-sharing plan to a class allocation (profit sharing/401k plan). This new plan will allow a tax deductible contribution of $42,000 which is approximately twice the amount he was able to deduct in

comparison to the old profit-sharing plan. The old plan required that all participants receive the same contribution, which restricted Jim from achieving the deductions he desired.

Speculation Stage:
- While Jim and Kathy needs to improve the base of their financial pyramid, they have already accumulated enough financial assets to allow themselves the option of speculating with a limited portion of those funds, if they are interested in doing so. They may begin to do this as they learn more about those options.

Summary:

Jim and Kathy's new plan succeeds in placing a protection barrier between their personal and business assets so that all of their personal and business assets are protected in the event of a lawsuit. With a majority of the college funding taken care of after the stock sale, they feel that they are on track for retirement. They have the ability to focus their discretionary dollars into their retirement plan. Kathy's additional income as a pharmacist was extremely helpful to supplement their savings program. By restructuring the profit-sharing/401k plan with Jim's practice, they were able to reduce their taxable income by doubling the amount he is able to contribute to the plan. Jim will continue to practice dentistry for several years and will start looking for potential buyers for his practice. They are confident that their new financial strategy secures their future retirement plans, and they look forward to a time when they will be able to double the length of their vacations overseas and spend much more time with their family.

Submitted by Brian W. Lahr

Case Study #4: The Jones...Married Couple with children

Circumstances: Ben & Allison, aged 38, have been busy raising a young family while balancing their careers, family and social demands. They recently moved into their second home which can easily accommodate a growing family...children's ages 8, 5, and 2. Ben & Allison don't have much spare time and their personal finances are often neglected. Recently Ben & Allison have decided to get their financial house in order. They are concerned they may not be on track to reach all of their goals. They are motivated to take action on several items. Two immediate priorities are preparing wills and planning for their children's upcoming college education. They are interested in developing a written financial plan to clarify the areas of deficiency and monitor future progress toward goals like education and retirement.

They have many future goals which include:

- paying 75% of three children's college educations
- retiring at age 60 with their current lifestyle
- ensure 401(k)'s, IRA's etc. are properly invested
- develop and monitor a written financial plan
- write a will
- prepare for the event of incapacity and/or death
- pay off several short-term debts

The Numbers:

Ben works as design engineer at a medical device company, and Allison works in IT at a local consulting firm. Their combined household income is $175,000. Both Ben and Allison have access to standard employee benefit packages including health insurance, disability insurance, life insurance, and 401K. Given their lifestyle they have the ability to save $2,200 per month.

Net Worth Statement:

Fixed Assets:
Savings Account:	$10,000
Checking Account:	$10,000
Total Fixed Assets:	$20,000

Variable Assets:
IRA:	$50,000
Roth IRA:	$40,000
Mutual Funds:	$5,000
Individual Stocks:	$10,000
Variable Life Cash Value:	$10,000
401k balance:	$40,000
Total Variable Assets:	$155,000

Personal and Other Assets:
Home:	$600,000
Vehicles:	$60,000
Personal Property:	$50,000
Total:	$710,000

Total Assets: $885,000

Liabilities:
Mortgage: (30 year @ 6%)	$480,000
Home Equity Line: (7%)	$95,000
Vehicle Loan: (9%)	$40,000
Credit Cards: (18%)	$5,000

Total Liabilities: $620,000

Net Worth: (Assets minus Liabilities) $265,000

Financial Planning Recommendations:

Security and Confidence Stage:
- Open a money market mutual fund. Maintain a 3-6 month expense reserve.
- Immediately pay off the credit cards
- Obtain supplemental individual long-term disability insurance to supplement both group plans at work.
- Obtain the maximum home equity line possible. Consider consolidating higher interest non-deductible consumer debt.
- Increase umbrella liability insurance to at least 1 million.
- Consider higher auto and home insurance deductibles.
- Obtain variable life insurance and term insurance in order to replace income, provide for final expenses, and future success of financial planning goals should either spouse prematurely die.
- Draft wills, trusts, and all other appropriate estate planning documents.

Capital Accumulation Stage:
- Open 529 plans for each child's education expenses.
- Aggressively contribute to Variable Life Insurance Policies.

Tax Advantaged Stage:
- Maximize 401(k) contributions.
- Maximize Roth IRA contributions while eligible (*modified adjusted gross income at $150,000 begins being phased out, total phase out at $160,000.*

Summary:

By developing a written financial plan, Ben & Allison were able to comprehensively understand their situation and have a common platform to communicate with their advisor. The Net Worth statement provided them a framework and a method of benchmarking future progress towards reaching their goals. In addition, the cash flow statement provided them an overview of their average income and expenditures, allowing for them to prioritize their spending. The retirement and education planning sections of the plan really helped answer their questions as to how they were progressing towards those important financial goals. Analyzing their entire portfolio allowed them to "x-ray" all of their investments and make sure the portfolio is efficient. Perhaps, the most helpful part of this process for Ben & Allison was the sense of relief they achieved knowing their insurance and estate plans are now implemented.

Submitted by Brad K. North

Case Study #5: The 53 year old early retirees

Circumstances: Larry has worked for the same company for 32 years. He never thought he could retire before age 62. They would like to so he and his wife Margie can enjoy their hobbies and spend time with their grandchildren.

Since most of Larry and Margie's net worth is in their company's private stock, they do not have much experience investing money and generating income from their investments.

They have many financial goals at this time:

- They want to know if they can retire at age 55.
- They want to know the benefits of working to age 57 when they get 100% of their medical benefits paid by the company.
- They want to know if they should diversify Larry's company stock.
- They want to know where their income will come from at retirement.
- They want to be sure they don't have to ever go back to work, because they are financially secure.

The Numbers:

Larry earns $55,000 per year and would like to retire at age 55 when he is eligible. He would like to replace 100% of his income at retirement but would like to spend some money right away on a new truck and take several trips with Margie.

If Larry works until age 57, his company will cover 100% of the cost of health insurance for both Larry and Margie.

Margie's mother is currently in poor health and Margie is concerned about needing to get some help taking care of her.

Larry's will get a $900 per month company pension.

Their Net Worth Statement

Fixed Assets:

Savings Account:	$5,000
Checking Account:	$3,000
Margie's IRA:	$22,000
Total Fixed Assets:	$30,000

Variable Assets:

Larry's 401k:	$88,000
Larry's company stock: (qualified)	$1,150,000
Total Variable Assets:	$1,238,000

Personal and Other Assets:

Home:	$380,000
Vehicles:	$30,000
Personal Property:	$60,000
Total:	$470,000

Total Assets:	$1,738,000

Liabilities:

Mortgage: (8 years left)	$98,000
Vehicle loan: (Margie)	$12,000
Total Liabilities:	$110,000

Net Worth: (Assets minus Liabilities)	$1,628,000

The Financial Plan:

Security and Confidence Stage:
- Secure individual long term care insurance
- Determine if Larry should replace group term life insurance with an individual policy (will depend on underwriting and what rate class he is approved in)
- Develop retirement projections to see how long their assets will last under a variety of circumstances and variables.
- Set up a plan to generate the annual retirement income without paying any pre-withdrawal penalties.
- If they decide on retiring earlier that age 57, then careful planning for picking up their medical insurance until then will be important.

Capital Accumulation Stage:
- Continue to defer income into the 401k plan until retirement
- Develop an investment policy statement which will be used as a guideline for the asset allocation decisions for managing all of their investments.

Tax Advantaged Stage
- Diversify the maximum 50% of the company stock into a portfolio of mutual funds, and variable annuities.

Summary:

Larry and Margie have too much risk with such a large position in the company stock. They are much more interested in preserving the assets they have than in generating high returns. If they decide to retire at Larry's age 55, they could access Larry's 401(k) plan to generate retirement income. They can consider diversifying some of the qualified company stock by either rolling it to an IRA, or taking an outright distribution, after evaluating the income tax consequences with their accountant. The IRA funds would be available to them after age 59 ½ without penalty.

The proceeds from the sale of company stock can be invested into several "buckets" that offer different levels of guarantees and growth potential. At retirement, Larry plans to diversify the majority of his company stock into several investments that can provide income including a fixed immediate annuity.

Submitted by Rich Hanzlik

Case Study #6: The Recently Widowed Woman

Jodi finds herself alone now, after her husband (Bill) passed away two months ago. His sudden heart attack at the age of 48 was not what they had planned. She has gone back to work part-time as a realtor, and is still struggling to get a handle on the finances and bills. They have two children, Laura is a junior at the local university, and Brad is a senior in high school. Jodi's financial goals are as follows:

- Maintaining the college funding for Laura and Brad
- Trying to learn about and make smart financial decisions on her own. She and Bill had always made decisions together.
- Structuring a plan that will invest the assets and life insurance proceeds to provide income for her now and for the rest of her life.

Her Net Worth Statement:

Fixed Assets:
    Savings Account: $10,000
    Money Market: $35,000
    Checking Account: $1,000
    Life Insurance Proceeds: $750,000
    Total Fixed Assets: $796,000

Variable Assets:
    IRA's: $56,000
    Mutual Funds: $200,000
    Individual Stocks: $317,000
    Variable Life Cash Value: $4,000
    Total Variable Assets: $577,000

Personal and Other Assets:
    Home: $425,000
    Vehicles: $50,000
    Personal Property: $100,000
    Total: $575,000

Total Assets: $2,173,000

Liabilities:
    Mortgage: $200,000
    Credit Cards: (Paid off monthly) $0
    Total Liabilities: $200,000

Net Worth: (Assets minus Liabilities) $1,748,000

The Financial Plan:

Security and Confidence Stage:
- Pay off the mortgage
- Purchase long term care insurance.
- Consider disability insurance if available based on income and health considerations.
- Increase the funding into her life insurance to be used as a long term tax deferred growth investment
- Draft wills, trusts, and appropriate estate planning documents.

Capital Accumulation Stage:
- Work with a financial advisor to begin selling most of the individual stocks (which Bill managed and Jodi has no interest in at all) to simplify the management of their assets.
- Initiate a fee-based brokerage account to start managing the mutual funds, stocks, and bonds and life insurance proceeds.
- Heavily fund Jodi's variable life policy for tax deferred growth, but keep it within the limits allowed by the IRS so that it doesn't turn into modified endowment contract.
- Fund a Roth IRA annually with the insurance proceeds in any year that she meets IRS eligibility limits.

Tax Advantaged Stage:
- Rollover Bill's 401(k) into an IRA for Jodi and manage it using a fee based brokerage account

Speculation Stage:
- Jodi should not utilize the Speculation stage at this time

Summary:

After working with a financial planner and better understanding her financial position, she found comfort in what she learned. The financial plan was a source of strength and comfort, not worry and stress. In addition, to work with a trusted advisor and have someone else to help her with the financial decisions was very helpful. Ultimately, she was able to simplify the management of the funds, set aside enough funds for college education, and generate a monthly income for her needs.

Submitted by Todd D. Bramson, CFP®, ChFC, CLU

11

Additional Resources

Glossary

Annuities, Fixed	An investment marketed by an insurance company that pays a guaranteed rate of return.
Annuity, Variable	An investment marketed by an insurance company with premiums mostly converted into separate accounts invested in stocks, bonds, and money market accounts.
Assets	An investment or property that has value.
	Those assets that do not have a major loss of principal. These would include the most conservative assets in your portfolio like checking and savings accounts, money market funds, certificates of deposit, T-bills, EE savings bonds, whole life insurance cash values.
"Bear" market	A period of time in which securities are declining in price.
"Bull" market	A period of time in which securities are rising in price.
Capital	Money or other assets.
Certificate of Deposit	An account at a bank, savings and loan, and/or credit union which pays a fixed rate over a certain period of time.

CFP®	A Certified Financial Planner™ is a person who advises others on achieving long-term financial goals, either for a fee or on a commission basis. Ethics and professional standards are monitored by the CFP® Board (www.cfp-board.org).
ChFC	Chartered Financial Consultant—a degree earned through the American College.
Debt	Owing money
Diversification	Spreading your risk amongst various accounts to reduce volatility.
Dollar Cost Averaging	The buying of a fixed dollar amount of stock shares at regular intervals so that more shares are bought at low prices, fewer at high, resulting in an average cost that is lower than the average price.
Inflation	A period of time marked by rising prices.
IRA	An Individual Retirement Account.
Liquidity	How easy is it to convert your investment into cash?
Money Market Mutual Fund	A pool of assets invested in bank CDs, T-Bills and commercial paper and considered the best emergency reserve account due to extreme safety and liquidity.
Portfolio	A listing of securities held by an investor or organization.
Principal	The current balance owed on a debt or the value of an account.
MSFS	Master of Financial Services. An advanced degree earned by the American College.

Mutual fund	A general term for an open-end investment company compromised of investments in basically any category.
Securities	Investments
Stock/share	A certificate representing ownership in a corporation that is usually sold to raise money to begin or expand a business.
T Bills	Treasury bill, a short-term federal obligation of the U.S. Treasury sold at a discount.

For Further Information:

The following is a very brief list of some of the resources for the individual interested in personal financial planning. To list all the helpful information available today would be a book in itself, so included here are some of the most popular and my personal favorites. The opinions and strategies expressed in the following sources should not be acted upon without first discussing them with a qualified investment, tax, and/or legal advisor.

Newspapers

The Wall Street Journal is the most widely read business newspaper. It also has daily articles about investing and money matters.

Barron's is a weekly newspaper that reviews the stock markets. The Lipper Analytical Services mutual fund performance ratings are included on a quarterly basis. There are also frequent articles on mutual fund investing

Investor's Business Daily is an excellent newspaper with a broad range of articles on finance, business and the economy.

New York Times and *USA Today* both have excellent business sections.

Magazines

Money magazine's December, January and February issues usually have articles on tax and investment planning.

Kiplinger's Personal Finance magazine's January issue focuses on financial planning (including tax planning) for the coming year. Mutual funds are reviewed in the September issue.

Smart Money offers articles on investing and financial planning.

Forbes is a bi-weekly investment magazine that looks at news from an investment point of view and has an annual mutual fund survey usually published in August.

Business Week focuses on current business news and contains articles on personal business, investing, and financial planning.

Books

Golf is Not a Game of Perfect by Bob Rotella has nothing to do with financial planning. But…since I'm addicted to the great sport of golf and am always trying to improve, and see others improve, I recommend this book any time I get a chance. It provides some great ideas on the mental side of the game.

The Millionnaire Next Door by Thomas Stanley provides an interesting look at wealthy people and their attitudes about money and life. You will be amazed that most millionaires are first generation and are frugal.

The New RetireMentality by Mitch Anthony is a great new book that identifies the issues facing everyone as they plan their future. This is especially helpful to those who are worried about what they will do during their retirement years.

There's No Place Like a Nursing Home by Karen Shoff is a must-read book for anyone who needs more education on long-term care for themselves or their loved ones.

The Ultimate Gift by Jim Stovall provides a very interesting story about wealth and the transfer of wealth to the next generation. I would suggest this book for anyone who wants to instill a sense of values and work ethic into their children, employees, etc.

Web sites

www.toddbramson.com is my Web site and has valuable links to many financial sites including many of those listed below

www.wallstreetcity.com has just about everything you need to know about stocks including free quotes, research, and criteria-based charts matching your specifications.

www.investorama.com lists information of thousands of online financial sites.

www.quicken.com includes a wealth of personal finance information as well as calculators and interactive financial formulas.

www.bloomberg.com offers financial market reports.

www.sec.gov is the official site of the Securities and Exchange Commission.

www.savingforcollege.com discusses the multitude of state 529 college plans available and each of their advantages.

www.morningstar.com features a comprehensive review of mutual funds, and portfolio tracking.

www.savingsbonds.gov lists everything you need to know about US Savings Bonds.

www.irs.gov provides information on the publications and forms for most tax questions.

ABOUT THE AUTHORS

Todd D. Bramson, CFP®, ChFC, CLU

Certified Financial Planner™, Todd D. Bramson, has been working in the field of financial planning for over 23 years and has been recognized as one of the 150 best financial advisors for doctors nationwide by Medical Economics. In fact, Todd was recently named as an editorial consultant to Medical Economics in the Tax and Personal Financial Planning area. Todd's first book, Real Life Financial Planning was published in June, 2004. This is the fifth in the series and the first book that includes case studies.

An exceptional teacher, motivating author, and speaker, he has been quoted in numerous financial publications and has spent several years as the financial expert on the local NBC live 5:00 p.m. news broadcast. In June of 2004, he spoke at the prestigious Million Dollar Round Table, a worldwide organization of the top 5 percent of all financial services professionals. He writes a quarterly e-newsletter called The Bramson Report and provides monthly teleseminars on timely financial subjects. See the following Web sites for more information on these resources.

www.toddbramson.com
www.asktoddbramson.com
www.yourwisdomresource.com

Todd's belief that "if the trust is there, the miles don't matter" has earned him devoted clients not only in his hometown of Madison, Wisconsin, but in almost every state in the country. Along with all the professional designations expected of a trusted financial professional, he is committed to keeping abreast of all the developments in his field and to playing an active role in his community. Bramson is active in his church, the Evans Scholars Alumni Foundation, and Blackhawk Country Club in Madison, WI.

North Star Resource Group
2945 Triverton Pike Drive #200
Madison, WI 53711
Direct: 1-608-271-3669 ext.218
Email: todd.bramson@northstarfinancial.com

Rich Hanzlik

Rich Hanzlik, Registered Representative, owns and operates Hanzlik Financial Services in Bayport, MN. He is a graduate of the University of Minnesota with a Bachelor of Science degree in Business Administration.

Since 1990, Rich has helped his clients identify their financial objectives and monitor the strategies during annual reviews. He specializes in helping clients make the emotional and stressful transition from a working career to a comfortable retirement.

He is a member of the National Association of Insurance and Financial Advisors (NAIFA), Million Dollar Round Table (MDRT) and has taught several continuing education classes and seminars in the financial services area.

Rich resides in Western Wisconsin with his wife and five children. His community activities revolve around Stillwater Lions club, Willow River Players community theatre and Relay for Life Cancer walk.

Hanzlik Financial
950 N. Hwy. 95
Bayport, MN 55003
Direct: 1-651-351-3776; Mobile: 1-651-233-0404
Email: rich@hanzlikfinancial.com

Jesse T. Karich

Jesse T. Karich came to North Star Resource Group from St. John's University in Collegeville, MN where he studied management and economics. Jesse specializes in working with physicians and small business owners to plan for their financial independence taking into account the specific needs of their chosen professions. He spends most of his time in Minneapolis, MN and Omaha, NE working with clients.

Jesse lives with his wife Jessica, yes Jessica, in Minneapolis, MN. When not meeting with clients he enjoys visiting his family's cabin near Ely, MN during the summer and fall months. You can also find Jesse on golf courses around the country trying to find his game.

North Star Resource Group
2701 University Ave. SE
Minneapolis, MN 55414
Direct: 1-612-617-6130; Toll Free: 1-888-404-8067
Omaha: 1-402-350-3637
Fax: 1612-256-3130
Email: Jesse.karich@northstarfinancial.com

Robert Kaufer

Robert Kaufer has over twelve years of experience as a practicing attorney working primarily in the areas of Simple and Complex Estate Planning, Business & Contract Law, Probate Law, and Residential Real Estate Law. Bob received his law degree from Hamline University School of Law and an MBA from The University of St. Thomas. He, his wife, and two children reside in St. Paul. Bob's legal philosophy is to educate the client about their options and then help them make the best choices to meet their unique goals and objectives. Robert is not affiliated with Marathon Advisors, Inc.

Phone: 1-612-508-4289
Website: www.kauferlaw.net
Email: bob@kauferlaw.net

Brian W. Lahr

Brian W. Lahr specializes in assisting Medical Professionals, Business Owners, and Successful Families in overcoming the financial challenges that are unique to their chosen career. Brian not only develops the financial plan, but also monitors the plan in periodic reviews so that it is always current. He strives to assist his clients in understanding alternatives that can enhance the efficiency and effectiveness of their money decisions.

Brian is a member of the Million Dollar Round Table (MDRT), The Premier Association of Financial Professionals® recognizing the top 5 percent of financial advisors worldwide. Brian has recently taken the role of Field Director at North Star where he allocates a portion of his time to growing and developing new advisors.

North Star Resource Group
2701 University Ave. SE
Minneapolis, MN 55414
Direct: 1-612-617-6043; Toll free: 1-877-213-8453
Iowa: 1-515-991-4841; Nebraska: 1-402-350-3637
Fax: 1-612-256-3043; Toll free fax: 1-877-239-7465
Email: brian.lahr@northstarfinancial.com

Brad K. North

Brad K. North, Financial Advisor; Associate Partner began his financial planning career in 1998, after graduating with a Bachelor's in Business Administration from the University of Wisconsin-Eau Claire. He is a member of the National Association of Insurance and Financial Advisors (NAIFA) and the Financial Planning Association (FPA) and is a perennial qualifier of the Million Dollar Round Table. He was also a featured advisor in the Morningstar™ 2006 Annual Survey

Brad provides fee-based comprehensive financial planning services through Marathon Advisors, Inc. and assists his clients with the development of a written financial plan. The plan is then monitored consistently and routinely so that it is always current. He is a specialist in retirement, investment college education, insurance, contingency-emergency, and estate planning.

Brad resides in Woodbury, Minnesota with his wife Anne, and sons Benjamin and Henry. Besides his family, he enjoys travel, music, including playing the guitar, running and golf.

North Star Resource Group
2701 University Ave. SE
Minneapolis, MN 55414
Direct: 1-612-617-6169
Fax: 1-612-617-6001
Email: brad.north@northstarfinancial.com

NORTH STAR RESOURCE GROUP

Marathon Advisors Inc. – *Investment Advisor Representative*
Registered Investment Advisor